PSYCHOLOGIC

PERSC

By
Avinash Kaur

ACKNOWLEDGEMENT

Writing this thesis has been fascinating and extremely rewarding. I would like to thank a number of people who have contributed to the final result in many different ways.

To commence with I pay my obeisance to God Almighty to have bestowed upon me good health, courage, inspiration and the light. I also express my sincere and deepest gratitude to my supervisor, Dr. Gurmeet Singh, Professor, Department of Physical Education, Punjab University, Chandigarh, who ploughed through several preliminary versions of my text, making critical suggestions and posing challenging questions. His expertise, invaluable guidance, constant encouragement, affectionate attitude, understanding, patience and healthy criticism added considerably to my experience. Without his continual inspiration, it would have not been possible to complete this study.

I owe my special thanks to the Chairman Dr. Th. Nandlal Singh, Professor Department of Physical Education, Panjab University, Chandigarh and the worthy faculty of the Department of Physical Education for their timely help and guidance.

I feel a deep sense of gratitude to my late parents, who formed part of my vision and taught me the good things that really matter in life.

I am extremely thankful to my dear friend Associate Professor Rajeshwarpal Kaur, who always encouraged and helped me during this research.

I choose this moment to acknowledge the great contribution of all the players who helped me to collected data for research.

I would like to record my gratitude to Principal Dr. Hardiljit Singh Gosal, who always inspired me to do Ph.D.

Words fail to express my appreciation to my family. I am overwhelmed and humble by my family's unwavering faith in my vision.

Finally I would like to thank everybody who was important to the successful realization of thesis.

Avinash Kaur

TABLE OF CONTENTS

LIST OF TABLES

LIST OF FIGURES

CHAPTER I

INTRODUCTION

In recent years, there has been an increasing amount of attention to the inter-relationships of personality variables and psychological characteristics with athletic performance. Most of this work has been concerned with delineating personality traits of athletes, differentiating among individuals by sports and level of success etc. Studies of measurement of personality traits of athletes and players are vital, if we are to secure the information needed by sport psychologists and coaches, who are charged with responsibility for selection, counselling and also the training of the athletes for competition. It is assumed that the personality structure correlates physical abilities as development of various personality traits such as sociability, confidence, emotional stabilisy, cooperativeness, personal adjustment and extraversion are entirely dependent upon the environment in which physical abilities are displayed (i.e. in sports and games) An ideal setting to enhance personal characteristics is provided by favourable environment where physical abilities are practiced and they are essential for increasing the athletic ability of the players and sports persons (Singh 1992).

Numerous physical, psychological and sociological factors influence the participation of an individual in modern sports. Development of motor skills involved and techniques and tactics of the game are the main areas to be focused upon besides the physical fitness and physique of the players, during his training usually the psychological factors are little emphasised upon for the performance of player at higher levels of competitive sports. The present study would be undertaken to investigate important psychological components of the sports-persons participating at different levels of competition.

In fact, the major dimension of the study of psychological aspect of sports is concerned with inquiries into the personality of sportsmen and sportswomen. There are numerous theories about the personality of athletes. But only a limited amount of research has been undertaken to support these theories. Several investigators have directed their attention towards an understanding of the relationship between personality and level of performance. Hence the relationship between participation in sport and personality is the most prevalent issue in sports personality.

1.1 SPORTS PERSONALITY

Personality though a highly ambiguous term is difficult to define and has become a useful concept in sports also. The term 'Personality' has a broad meaning. Besides physical, it also includes psychological and social characteristics of the individual. The origin of the word, 'personality' could be traced to Latin language where word 'persona' means 'mask' indicating the cover worn to depict various drama characters by actors in ancient plays and the personality of the individual was judged by the outer appearance. At that time, this word was used to refer to the roles played by the individual and the impression others got of him. Persona being something external in nature which excludes the inner traits of individual, it is considered as a narrow concept.

However, with the passage of time, it has gained a broader sense in terms of sum total of characteristics, which indicates how a man will behave under particular situations. Hence the personality of individual is judged on the basis of the ways he interacts with other people in various situations and in turn, how the other people view him. Generally speaking, personality is regarded as a collection of traits, which everyone is said to possess to a greater or a lesser degree.

Human personality is so complex a phenomenon that it can be interpreted in many ways. The notion of mask approach is that the personality was assumed to be the influence and impact upon the audience that individual wearing the mask has left. Personality means the effect which an individual leaves on other people. According to this conviction the externality of an individual i.e. the facial expression, gestures, movements, manners, physique etc. constitutes personality, gestures, physique etc. Here the emphasis is on the superfluity of an individual. According to this view, personality would refer to the way a person appears and affects others and also the way he stimulates others, i.e. his social stimulus value. Hence it is conceptualized that personality is the integration and organization of multiple human traits.

Personality is an amalgamation of relatively persistant behaviour responses which indicates reaction of person to the environment. Personality is the way someone behaves over a long period and in a variety of situations. Personality characterizes individuals as they appear in most circumstances. The individual's behaviour is greatly governed by social factors. These social factors give a definite shape to a person's individuality and as a result of it, his personality develops.

Psychologically, the physical, mental, social and moral characteristics of an individual in dynamic organization constitutes personality manifested in social life integrated. It includes both his emotional and attitudinal traits. So it is the total being of man, It refers to one's total make-up i.e.; biological as well as sociological. His physique and chemique, his emotionality, his intelligence, his character, his sociability all make up his personality. According to the conviction here, approves the personality as aggregate of social, physical, temperamental, mental and social build up of an individual and ideals, attitudes, interest, aptitude, intelligence, experience, habits, perception, memory, imagination and various ways of behaviour.

The substance approach of personality centers round the underlying nature of the person i.e. the basic determiners of the behaviour patterns which are the characteristics of him, such as forces, motives, systems, mechanisms, processes and structures which cannot be observed directly. Persona approach of personality implies the false appearance, front, showy but deceptive nature; but the substance approach means the true character of the individual which is the individual's intrinsic nature and that is the supreme reality which regulates his visible behaviour.

1.1.1 PERSONALITY DEFINED

Historically the correlation of sports performance and personality is the most desirable issues in sports personology performance. Personality though a highly ambiguous term is difficult to define. The interaction of social and physical world with biological organism frames the personality which marks individuality. A man's real personality includes what he wishes to be, how he wishes to appear, how he appears to others and how he appears to himself. It involves evaluation of his environment, of other people and of himself. According to functional explanation, "Personality is aggregate virtue of individual's behaviour depicted in his interests, attitude, thinking process, manner of act and personal ideology of existence.

Different authors have defined personality in different ways.Allport (1937) in an exhaustive survey of the literature, examined almost some fifty definitions of personality. After comprehensive summary and evaluation, Allport strived to integrate supreme elements of previous definitions and ignoring their flows and constructed his concept of pesonality. He suggested that personality may be defined as "what a man really is." However, realizing that this is too abbreviated a definition of personality which is inadequate to encompass the entirety of personality, he proceeded to suggest his incorporated definition.

He defines personality as the strong organization within the individual of those psychophysical systems that determine his unique adjustment with his social environment. Later on, in a 1961 revision of his major work, he somewhat modified his personality definition by substituting a new phrase "characteristic behaviour and thought" for the previous "unique adjustment to his environment". It means that it determines his characteristic behaviour and thought. Thus, Allport (1961) recast his definition as "We not only adjust to our environment but we reflect on it. Also we strive to master it and sometimes we succeed.Behaviour and thought, therefore, make both for "survival and for growth". He emphasized on the individuality of personality and went to a considerable length in theorizing to state and said, "No two people think or behave alike." Such a view is crucial for understanding behaviour in sports.

Guilford (1959) simply defines it he empmhasized on uniqueness of each individual. As everyone behaves acts or adjusts to situations differently, the individuals vary in their systematic coordination and integration of personality traits. In his opinion, the best way to understand personality is by comparing the differences among people.

Eysenck (1960) believes that "personality is more or less stable and enduring organisation of a person's character, temperament, intellect and physique, which determines his unique adjustment to the environment." Besides supporting the notion of adjustment and uniqueness, he also adds two terms,' "character and temperament". Character implies that a particular code of behaviour exists in people's actions. It is only to a kind of personality one has that makes the character 'good' or bad'. Temperament refers to biological and physiological disposition, a person has towards events. It refers to emotional nature.

Cattell (1965) has defined personality as 'that which tells what a man will do when placed in a given situation."

Personality, according to Eysenck (1968), is a steady and enduring organization of an individual's character, temperaments, intellect and physique which describes about the physiological differences between introverts and extroverts in the light of concept of weak and strong nervous system.

Alderman (1974) defines personality as "an integration or merging of all the parts of one's psychological life---the way one thinks, feels, acts and behaves." He suggests that personality has two fold: feeling and thinking on one side while behaving acting on other side.

Walten M. Schell (1976) mentioned both inner and outer processes and which of these emphasized behaviour. According to him, personality consists of "the different patterns of behaviour (including thoughts and emotions) that characterize each individual's adaptation to the situation of his or her life."

A very comprehensive definition of personality has been given by Maddi (1976) who more extensively defines personality as a stable set of traits and tendencies that determine those commonalities and differences in the psychological behaviour (thought, feelings, and actions) of people that have continuity in time and that may or may not be easily understood in terms of the social and biological pressures of the existent situation alone". He stresses on similarities and differences that exist in people. This is possible only through observing people's actions and behaviour under certain conditions.

The personality of an individual is depiction of his behaviour, which is made up of many components, some of which are objective and therefore, easily studied and measured. And some are subjective and cannot be measured easily. These objectives components are physique, speed, strength and movement. The subjective components include motives, feelings, ideas, attitudes, character, will-power etc.

No significant none of the definition is acceptable to all the psychologists but they agree that personality constitutes individual's behaviour patterns exhibited across circumstances or all those psychological characteristics that might have led to such pattern of behaviour. Various approaches are chosen by researchers studying personality depending upon definition they follow. Although the various definitions of personality do serve the purpose of operationalizing variables for study, they do not, unfortunately provide a consensual definition of personality.

Levy (1970) has conceptualized his own approach to understanding personality and offered a model that identifies components common to most of all specific definitions of personality. He states that the concept of personality is based upon three conditions;

(i) By nature personality comprises of behaviour depending upon features that define significant of aspect of individual's identify that might be labelled as needs, motives or cognition,

(ii) Personality deals with behaviour which is either affected by internal locus of control or the one which cannot be elaborated in terms of the circumstances prevailing in external environment.

(iii) A certain degree of organized structure where numerous human behaviours seems to fit into significant pattern must be possessed in this behaviour.

1.1.2 ROLE OF PERSONALITY IN SPORTS

The physical educator and a coach becomes interested in psychological studies because of the belief that personality plays a role in the selection and participation in physical activities and sports.Moreover,the involvement in physical education and sports contributes to personal and social adjustment. The development of personality and the achievement of desirable social values have been the objectives of sports and physical education since early times. The findings that the athletes are different from non-athletes may not mean that athletics cause enhanced personality characteristics. It may be that athletics and sports produce the more well-adjusted individuals in society or it helps in removing maladjustment.

Although most sport personality research has focused on the description of personality characteristics in athletes and the influence of personality on sports behaviour, the study of the effects of sports participation on personality development and change has also been an important area of research. It seems logical to consider that various personality characteristics (e.g; competitiveness, self-confidence) are important to achieving success in sports. Another idea is that the sports participation modifies or develops some significant personality attributes (e.g. emotional control, self-esteem) i.e; participation in sports and physical activities enhances psychological and physical development. Both of these issues have been extensively investigated over the last four decades. Fisher (1984) found that well over one thousand studies have been conducted on personality and sports behaviour.

Personality has encountered utmost attention in recent years in the field of sports psychology and athletic behaviour. "Personality" is a term commonly used by people concerned with almost every aspect of human interaction. A coach evaluating an athlete will often refer to his or her personality. Rushall (1970) has admitted regarding the importance of personality in athletic performance. He also feels that "knowledge of the personality of an individual is important for maximizing individual responses." He further says that

(i) if a relationship between personality and physical performance exists, one could differentiate, for selective purposes, between players of equal skill, and

(ii) repeated testing of players gives an indication of change in athletes. The coach can then readjust his player control procedures to these changes.

Singer (1972) had also opined similarly. Since personality is determined by genetic factors but modified by environmental experiences, a strong possibility exists that personality influences activity-preferences and as well as gets modified by activity experiences. The personality mould is formed early in life but can be changed by later experiences partly, if not completely. He has suggested that an individual has both basic personality traits and an external personality. It is our external personality that determines how others see us. We are all concerned about how others perceive us and this may be particularly true of athletes who are so constantly in the public eye. Though external traits are not necessarily indicative of deeper traits, it is external trait that coaches are most likely to perceive and most likely to affect. Singer has suggested that there are some personality traits, which are inherited while some are nurtured by society. These traits as a group make up the individual or the "real "person.

Sperling (1942) found that the performance in sports correlates personality variables of players, extraversion and neuroticism seems to greatly influence sports performance. For instance extraversion was highly supportive to sociability and dominance in athletes and sports participants (Gotheil and Werner 1966).

In neuroticism, the individual suffers extreme sadness and defection during some distressing stress situation. The extreme level of anxiety and apprehensiveness along with reduced activity and loss of initiative is seen in neurotic individual. Eysenck (1967) suggested association of neuroticism, stability with hypothalamus.

As personality is reflective of the entire behavioural dimensions of individuals, it has a strong bearing not only on athletic preferences but it has a direct link with sports performance. Tutko and Richards (1971) had long ago identified various personality traits such as intelligence, organization, leadership, coachability, emotionality, mental toughness, trust, responsibility, developing conscience, aggression are hghly related to good athletic achievement.

1.1.3 STRUCTURE OF PERSONALITY

Hollander (1967) has stated that "Personality is characteristics or mingle of characteristics making an individual unique. Hence personality is referred to each person's uniqueness. It also includes a person's values, interests, motives and many other factors. A socially competent person requires the development of socially approved personality dispositions. Moreover; attitudes and personality are related concepts. Attitudes and values form important dimensions of personality.Personaliy components determine the development and change of attitudes.

How personality factors may influence participation and performance? How participation in physical activities and sports determines the influence on the personality? Another approach or model for understanding personality is conceptualized by Hollander (1967). According to him, personality may be viewed at three distinct levels and along two dimensions. He incorporates the peripheral and vital personality structure into a model which embraces role-related behaviour, the psychological core, social environment and the typical responses. His model of personality is internal yet exhibited externally, persistent yet dynamic, and intrapersonal though affected by social environment. According to him, personality structure is divided into three inseperable levels i.e. (i) psychological core (ii) typical responses (iii) behaviour related to role and two dimensions.

A schematic view of Personality Structure

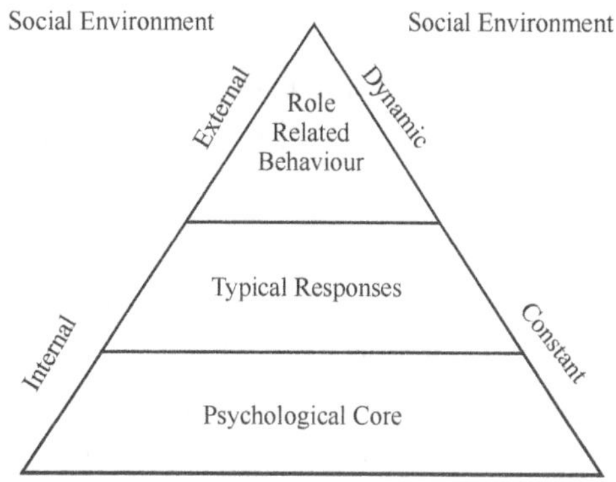

(Adapted from Martens 1975) Hollander's model of Personality.

The triangle in the above figure represents an individual's personality in relation to the social environment within which the person functions. The external-internal and dynamic-constant dimensions of the personality are represented by two sides of the triangle. For both dimensions, the density of the lines represents the permeability that each level of personality has with respect to the social environment. The wary lines between the three levels of personality illustrate that the three levels are closely interrelated.

PSYCHOLOGICAL CORE

The psychological core is the most rudimentary level of personality as it involves the values, belief, attitudes, interiors and notions about our self and our worth. It is the real self and the most prominent part of personality dealing with what we are instead of what we want others to think of us for instance our moral values might revolve around the significance of friends, family and religion in our life. It is the most stable and unchanging part of personality. (e.g., Allport, 1937; Eysenck, 1960; Maddi, 1976). This foremost level is completely based upon our perception about our self and of external world and our interaction with surrounding world i.e. social life. Hollander assumes the self concept as centre piece of this core. It is at the internal level.

TYPICAL RESPONSES

The way we learn the adjustment with the environment and how we respond to situations and circumstances around us constitutes around constitutes typical responses. The personality core is reflected by typical responses. For instance, if you respond to external situations by being shy, you are likely to be called introvent though you might be shy, happy-go-lucky and short-tempered at times. They are fairly predictable behaviours that emanate from our core characteristics. They are learned modes of adjustment to the environment. They are external or at behavioural level. The personologist refers to characteristic manner in responding to such things as frustration, humour and anxieties.

1.1.4 ROLE- RELATED BEHAVIOUR

The upper part in the model represents role-related behaviours which we engage in daily, based upon the influence of the social environment. The dynamic aspect of our personality is depicted by behaviour related to role as they deal with behavoiurs which are situationally changing. Our action is based upon our perception of social situation. This is known as Role-Related behavour. It is the most dynamic aspect of individual's personality: the environment change triggers our perception and it changes are behaviour. Dissimilar situation demands different roles to be played as on same day, we perform numerous roles as of student, employee, friend, mother or coach etc. sometimes our roles might conflict with one another e.g. a parent coaching the team of his/her child might feel clash between her parenting and coaching roles.

The external features of personality dependent upon the societal environment and change, whereas the internal features are more stable. The dynamic component allows for changes based on learning and the stability part provides a well formed structure to individual for proper functioning in society.

1.1.5 WHY STUDY PERSONALITY STRUCTURE?

The fundamental level i.e. the psychological core is most internal, hardest but stable component of personality, which remains static over time while role related behaviour is utmost dynamic and external that is greatly affected by environment around us i.e. social. As our responses are the result of psychological core and behaviour related to roles so they might lie somewhere in between. Stability with dynamism is integral part of personality. While the stability component provides an organized structure to function, the dynamic aspect help in new learning (when bug & Gould, 2003). The interaction of psychological core, typical responses and social characteristic of sports allows prediction of role-related behaviour. (e.g., public evaluation, salient rewards etc,)

The psychological core might include an individual's self-concept, perceived ability in relation to sports, and achievement goal orientations. These basic underlying personality foundations would then influence various typical responses or traits/dispositions of the individual, such as self-confidence, competitive trait anxiety and locus of control. The individual's role-related behaviours would be influenced by the trickle-down of core and dispositional characteristics as well as the specific situational influences on behaviour at that moment. Role-related behaviours might be competitive state anxiety, cognitive strategies, physiological manifestations of stress and performance.

As coaches and physical trainers, we can be more effective when we understand the different levels of personality formation that lie beyond the role-related behaviours particular to a circumstance. As sports psychologists, we have to understand the different levels of personality structures. Getting to know the actual person (i.e. the psychological core) and that person's typical modes of responses produces insight into the individual's motivations, actions and behaviour. Although personality very much broad to be defined in one specific way, theorists such as Hollander (1967) and Levy (1970) have provided useful models of personality that may work as frameworks for the organized study of personality in sport.

1.2. LOCUS OF CONTROL

Another personality aspect to be evaluated for sports-persons is the locus of control. LOC refers to the extent to which a person believe he can control events affecting him/ her. The roots of the concept could be traced back to Julian B. Rotter who developed it in 1954.

The word 'Locus' is used in Latin language for 'place' or 'location' which can either be internal (when person feel they can control their life events) or external (when the cause of event is attributed to external environment, some supreme powers or other people controlling their life and decisions).

Some people who feel themselves to be responsible for things happening to them are labelled as internals. People with high LOC believe events a result of their own actions and behavoiur. While others who find their life outcomes to be influenced by forces beyond control (i.e. fate, luck or other people) are labelled as externals.

Rotter (1966) gave the concept of 'Locus of Control' while proposing his thought of social learning. Constructing LOC is the dimension of personality that deals with individual's perception of events occurring in life. The achievement oriented behaviour is inseperable from locus of control. Rotter labels persons as 'internal' who feel that they can control the destinies while 'externals' are those who believe the outcomes in life are result of some outside forces, internals are better adjusted and much happier in their life than externals.

The individual with internal LOC approves his/ her life guided by personal attempts and decisions while those with external LOC attributes the outcomes in life to some external forces such as chance, fate, luck, other people or some external circumstances.

One should trust his/ her own abilities to achieve high and earn satisfaction. The LOC influence the perception of people regarding how they view outcomes, the world, the identification causes success or failure.

Internal cause refers to personal while external are known to be situational ones. Most of the people fall in mid of these two extremes and forms persistent division of beliefs of locus of control. Although LOC is comparatively enduring temperamental feature which is highly modifiable by experience.

The LOC characteristic is supreme in understanding the notion of learning procedure in comparatively variant learning situation. The construction of LOC is an intrinsic component of Rotter's (1954) theory of social learning that provides theoretical grounds for his belief of nature and impact of reinforcement and his work on numerous expectancy levels.

The interaction of an individual with his meaningful surrounding is the unit of comprehensive study of personality. The personality theorists identifies behaviour as directional aspect deduced from effect of reinforcement. The depiction of the behaviour of person is attributed to nature, importance of aim, the reinforcements as well as person's own expectation that goal might occur. Therefore, the potential behaviour expectancy level and the value of reinforcement constructs the social learning theory of Rotter.

1.2.1 INTERNAL AND EXTERNAL LOCUS OF CONTROL

Rotter (1966) concept of LOC a component describing personality related to perception of individual regarding relations between results controlled by the behavoiur and its reinforcement. The internal LOC is the intensity to which individual attributes his own behaviour leading to outcome, as suggested by Rotter (1990).

The individuals with higher internal LOC can regulate their actions, tend to display much political behavoiurs and have tendency to influence those with lower LOC. Such people more tend to believe in notion that their actions and work will help them reach goal. They quickly seek information and knowledge about situations and view their future in their own hands.

Their confidence in belief of making the things change by own efforts help them in influencing people and situations. Such individuals are more achievement oriented and may be politically active.

They are more distinct, less generalize and find uniqueness in each situation. The people in the middle have highest internal LOC but the stumbling block is such individual tend to accept the same quickly for their failures too. The individuals with higher external LOC attribute the outcomes of their action to situations and other people totally outside their control. Such people find themselves entrapped in a situation such a way that they are left with no other option but to obey what is happening to them.

The extent to which people assign the outcome of event to matter of luck, chance or which are not under their control or are unpredictable is described as external LOC by Rotter (1990)

People with higher external LOC are fatalistic in observing the surrounding or circumstances and feel helpless in what is happening. Such beliefs make them more passive and depressed. They perceive similar situations as likely to have same consequences and hence they step back without working for it. Not only this, they attribute their success to luck instead of hard work. The older and young people tend to develop higher external LOC.

It must be noticed that the internals cannot always be regarded 'good' and external to be equivalent 'bad'. The concept of LOC differs with situations.

For instance, individual terrible at sports might get depressed upon this performance. If he had strong internal LOC, he might develop an attitude of 'I don't try that hard enough and I failed resulting into stressed feeling. While person with strong external LOC states "The game is too hard" or "My team mates didn't cooperate". They will probably be more comfortable and released.

LOC is a variable that labels the individual as 'external' or 'internal' depending upon the feeling of control over outcome (Phares 1968) these differences among the individuals occurs due to perception of outcome attributed to own efforts or to luck fate or uncontrollable external forces.

Thus, the LOC is personality variable depending upon expectancies regarding self control over the reinforcement that will with follow the effort or behavoiur of individual.

Various researchers such as (Franklin 1963, Chance 1965) found the internals to be more dynamic in the intellectual spheres while others found non-significant relation between LOC and intelligent quotient. Supported healthy relation between internal LOC and IQ. The gifted children in India and Iran are not different significantly from mean on I.E., total and the three sub scales i.e. Academic, Leadership success and Luck-fate but significant difference was found between the gifted and average children on politics and personal respect, where the gifted are more 'external'.

The perception of one's control over all those things which might influence us seems to be psychologically healthy as internal LOC is regarded desirable. Internal locus of control could develop "personal control", "Self-agency" and "Self-determination".

1.2.2. ORIGIN OF THE CONCEPT

Rotter's (1954) social learning theory finds fundamental unit in locus of control concept. James and Phares (1950) worked upon expectancies of LOC in its infancy. The two types of expectancy shifts as studied by William H. James are:

- typical expectancy shifts- believe that the failure or success would be followed by same outcome.
- Atypical expectancy shift-belief that dissimilar outcome follows success or failure.

The researchers working on it found people who tend to show typical expectancy shift attribute their outcomes to own ability while those depicting atypical expectancy assigned their outcome to chance. Such work divided people into those who attribute to ability (internal cause) versus all those who attributes to luck (external cause)

1.2.3. LOCUS OF CONTROL IN SPORTS

LOC is personality variable of expectancy describing the perception of control that an individual has over the reinforcement or outcome which follow his behaviour. The performance, either good or poor, is not considered to be matter of luck or fate by people on higher LOC, the external LOC people tends to explain the events of their lives as result of fate, chance, luck or powers of other people.

The belief of control over the reinforcement experienced by person creates the individual differences. Forces of fate, chance, power of others, complexities of world are looked upon by those with external LOC and such people tend to believe in forces beyond their control. Those who feel like controlling the future themselves and considers themselves responsible for occurrence of any event are referred as having internal LOC.

Most people have some qualities of both external and internal control, but tend to view the predominately more from one perspective or the other.

The players with internal or external LOC also influence the performance. People of internal LOC are more motived for achievement and hence are goal oriented while with external LOC fears the failure and attribute outcome to chance. Internal raise goal after success and lowers slightly after a failure while externals set extremely high or low goals and are risk lowers.

The athletes who explain the events in their lives i.e. reward or punishment as a result of some external forces such as fate, luck, chance or power to others are described as external controls. On the other side the athletes with internal controls attribute the events or their life as an outcome of their own behaviour.

Athletes might believe that their success or failure chances are influenced by some internal or external causes. The accomplishments are the result of personal effort is a belief possessed by athlete with internal LOC. While the athlete with external LOC views the situation as outcome of chance variable. Such athlete's performance is affected by luck, environmental factors and few other societal variables.

Many athletes possess the quality of both internal and external LOC. The good athletes often tend to be more internal as they believes in the notion that efforts and capability would only give them success. Internal tend to achieve more than the externals in life as they are more persistent who can even delay the gratification of rewards and their reaction towards the failure is less negative.

The outside forces are given much emphasis by athletes with external control and they can never derive personal satisfaction even when experienced success. Some unrealistic high or low goals are set by them and they might take unnecessary risk. The internalization process of the motivation is emphasised upon by internal control athletes whereas the identification methods influence externals.

The internals are more desirable and their coaches must try to develop following characteristics:-

(1) The coaches must help the athletes to experience such situations where their personal efforts will produce the desired results.

(2) The athletes must be taught to set realistic goals and must take personal responsibility for their behavour.

Personal Causation:

Some people develop the feeling that they are net in control of themselves or their destiny. The extreme dependence upon others for the direction might be a way of life style for some. They develop a feeling that whatever happens to them is beyond their personal control and their achievement is the result of fate, chance or others.

The perceived locus of causality explains the term personal causation. The two extreme types of individuals are (i) origins and (ii) Pawns.

(1) The one's who experience being an origin view themselves as originating and developing their own behaviour. They seem to have it all together needing something of personal meaning. Example- (a) Understanding the features of prominent situation. (b) Analysing what to do (c) Performing appropriate actions (d) Being successful and (e) feeling causation that they themselves originated their action.

(2) Pawns believe themselves to be pushed around and being doomed for the failure. They are certainly not as inadequate to the extent they can't be worked with for changing their attitudes and beliefs. Pawns can be converted to origins with resourceful training.

1.3. NEED OF THE STUDY

The researchers in the sports personology have expressed been desire to frame a comprehensive psychological characteristics for improving sports standards. Now a days there is a great race to win medals. Psychological factors were identified as important factors responsible for excelling in sports.

Athletics and sports require not only physical fitness, but top level sports depend on psychological adjustment, social and emotional maturity and many other psychological characteristics. Psychological factors help physical educators and coaches to understand the reality of fitness and personality traits of the players before and during competition. Personality of the players which influences the performance is also affected by many other factors like anxiety, will to win, aggressiveness, fear and attitude. No doubt, the present study will help the coaches and researchers to improve the psychological traits of athletes in modern age.

According to Mohan, (1989), personality has a remarkable importance in sports psychology because it is the core of individual difference and has its bearing on human performance. The knowledge of personality of sportspersons when made available to the sport psychologists can be very useful to achieve excellence in sports. The present study would be helpful in selection of athletes for different sports, in according with the identified personality traits needed in different sports and games. Training programs can also be monitored on the basis of such personality data available for them.

Hence there is a dire need to study the psychological characteristics like different personality traits, such as sociability, dominance, extraversion, self-concept, conventionality, mental toughness and emotional stability as well as locus of control of sports-persons both males and (females) participating at school, college and university levels and also to make comparison of the same psychological characteristics of the sports-persons of individual and team games as well as between male and female athletes of different games separately and combined.

1.4. STATEMENT OF THE PROBLEM

The problem was entitled as below:

"SELECTED PSYCHOLOGICAL CHARACTERISTICS OF SPORTS PERSONS AT DIFFERENT LEVELS OF PARTICIPATION".

1.5. OBJECTIVES OF THE STUDY

The objectives of the present study are given below:-

1. To measure the personality characteristics, like sociability, dominance, extraversion, self-concept, conventionality, mental toughness and emotional stability as well as the internal and external locus of control of the female athletes participating at inter college and inter university levels.
2. To know the differences on sociability, dominance, extraversion, self-concept, conventionality, mental toughness and emotional stability of personality and locus of control among the female athletes.
3. To make comparison of sociability, dominance, extraversion, self-concept, conventionality, mental toughness and emotional stability of personality and locus of control between female athletes of ball games and combat sports at inter college and inter university levels of competition.
4. To establish relationship among the different components of all these variables for female athletes at inter college and inter university levels.
5. To find out the differences on the dominance, sociability, extraversion, conventionality, self-concept, mental toughness and emotional stability between the female athletes with external and internal locus of control.

1.6. HYPOTHESES OF THE STUDY

In order to achieve stipulated objectives, the following hypotheses of the present study would be framed:

1. There would be significant differences on sociability, dominance, extraversion, self-concept, conventionality, mental toughness and emotional stability and locus of control among the female athletes of inter college and inter university levels of competition.

2. There would be significant differences on sociability, dominance, extraversion, self- concept, conventionality, mental toughness and emotional stability and locus of control among the female athletes of three games at inter college and inter university levels of competition.

3. There would be significant differences on sociability, dominance, extraversion, self- concept, conventionality, mental toughness and emotional stability and locus of control between the female athletes of ball games and combat sports.

4. It is predicted that significant relationship would exist among the dominance, sociability, self-concept, extraversion, conventionality, mental toughness and emotional stability of the female athletes of different games.

5. It is assumed that significant differences would exist on seven psychological characteristics among the female athletes with external and internal locus of control.

1.7. DELIMITATIONS OF THE STUDY

The present study was delimited as follows:

1. Only a few psychological characteristics would be studied in the present study; e.g.; sociability, dominance, extraversion self-concept, conventionality, mental toughness and emotional stability and locus of control.

2. The sample of the study was confined to 600 female sportspersons from ball games i.e. (300) and combat sports i.e. also (300).

3. An attempt was made to take female subjects equally from ball games and combat sports.

4. The sample of sports persons would be selected both from ball games as well as combat sports.

5. The players of team games i.e. Baseball, Football and Handball and combat sports would be from Judo, Taekwondo and Wrestling for the study.

1.8. LIMITATIONS OF THE STUDY

Following are the limitations of the present study:-

1. The questionnaire for research has its own limitations. Any bias that may enter into the response of the subject of this account may be considered as the limitation of the study.

2. The investigator was unable to control the other variables such as home environment, daily routine, diet etc. which was again a limitation of the study.

1.9. DEFINITIONS / EXPLANATION OF THE TERMS USED

1. PSYCHOLOGICAL CHARACTERISTICS:

In the present study the seven personality traits of the sports-persons would be used; e.g. sociability, dominance, extraversion, self-concept, conventionality, mental toughness and emotional stability

1. **Sociability** means a sociable person is warm, easy going, good-natured, attentive to people, ready to cooperate, trustworthy, soft-hearted, kind, adaptable and warm-hearted. It is an important trait for athletes in that it implies being generous to team-mates and that criticism from others will be accepted in good faith (Singh and Cheema 2005).

2. **Dominance** indicates hardness, self-assertiveness, self-assurance, and toughness, persuading, unconventionality and competitive aggressiveness, seducing or commanding others. Dominance is characterized by desire to influence and control one's environment and other people and is linked with ability for directing and controlling other people through subduing, persuading, seducing or commanding them (Singh and Cheema 2005).

3. **Extraversion** means outgoing, uninhibited, impulsive, sociable, friendly, craving for excitement, and having many social contacts. They are aggressive, optimistic, laugh a great deal, lose their temper easily and act at spur of the moment are unable to keep their feelings under control. (Singh and Cheema 2005)

4. **Self-concept** reflects several kinds of identifiable personality traits such as self-assurance, self-esteem, self-confidence, self-consistency, self-assertiveness, self-

enhancement, self-regard and self-respect. What a person perceives of himself and his achievement in life is called self-concept. Self-confidence and self-assurance in athletes are expressed in behaviour as cheerful, resilience, toughness, placidity, experience, carelessness, vigour, energy, fearlessness and self-security. (Singh and Cheema 2005)

5. **Conventionality** denotes behaviour such as being alert to proper ways of doing things, being very practical, narrowing of interests to immediate problems, being realistic, dependable, sound, being concerned and worried about issues. Many researchers have found athletes to be highly conservative and conventional in their responses to social situations. (Singh and Cheema 2005)

6. **Mental Toughness** indicates characteristic of an athlete who can take rough handling; do not easily upset about losing, playing badly or being spoken to rudely, can accept strong criticism without being hurt and do not need too much encouragement from their coaches. This is also manifested in realistic, self-reliant, and cynical behaviour. Cattell (1960) described the tough-minded individual as one who is emotionally mature, independent in action and thought, hard and realistic in his appraisal of himself and the world can overrule his feelings and does not show anxiety about events occurring about him. (Singh and Cheema 2005)

7. **Emotional Stability** is characterized by maturity, placidness, absence of neurotic fatigue, unaffectedness, stability quiet realism, optimism and self-discipline. While on the other hand, emotional instability is characterized by low tolerance of frustration, immaturity, instability, high excitability, evasiveness and neurotic fatigability. There is a high level of anxiety and apprehensiveness, together with diminished activity, lowered self-confidence and a general loss of initiative. (Singh and Cheema 2005)

II. LOCUS OF CONTROL:

The construct of locus of control is an expectancy variable of personality requiring an individual's perception of controlling over events occurring in his life. People have internal or external locus of control. Persons with an internal locus of control tend to believe that his behaviour influence results and performances in his life, whereas those with an external locus of control assign outcomes to outside forces such as fate, chance, destiny and other people. (Husnain. N & Joshi D.D. 1992)

III. SPORTS PERSONS:

These are those students who have been playing some sports for several years and who have been selected to participate in some competition at inter college or inter university levels contests.

1.10. SIGNIFICANCE OF THE STUDY

There exists relationship between the personality variables and sports performance. Sports psychologists and coaches are interested in the measurement of personality traits of athletes and players, which has become an important area of study of psychological aspects of sports. Personality plays a role in the selection and participation in physical activities and sports. The development of personality and achievement of desirable social values have been the objectives of sports and physical education since early times, as sports produce the more well-adjusted individuals in society.

It goes without saying that the elite athlete emerges out of thousands of sports participants. There is an ample evidence available in the developed countries that from the 'mass' participation, a 'class one participation emanates. The picture, however, has been different in country like, India where comparatively few people participate in sports notwithstanding a huge population of the country. However, with the passage of time, the developing countries have started realizing the importance of mass participation in sports. As far as the development of sports excellence out of mass participation is concerned, the participants who are to be groomed as future stars of sports, definitely need scientific backing in the form of specific assessment, guidance and counselling. For example, if we know the fitness indices of a particular young population, they can be guided accordingly to become future athletes.

Apart from the earlier practical significance, the present investigation would also throw light on the linkage between psychological parameters and physical performance in relation to the athletic and non-athletic grouping, age groups and the type of domicile of the athletes. With this, the investigation at -hand can be viewed as having both theoretical and practical implications in the field of sports.

CHAPTER II

REVIEW OF RELATED LITERATURE

The comprehensive review of the research related theme of study is vital pre-requisite to detailed planning and execution of any research work before commencement of fresh study. The information and analysis of results of any research study gets accumulated in the form of encyclopedias, books, journals, abstracts, thesis and other published forms over a period of time. Realizing the importance of review, Best (2008) says, "A familiarity with the literature in any problem area helps the students to discover what is already known and what is still unknown and untested."

The investigation could be successfully done by avoiding the duplication only by detailed study of related literature. Moreover it taken the researcher familiar to stages involved in research. Without the knowledge of what others have done n related research and what still needs to be done, the development of a research project is not possible such studies contributes in the form of theories, ideas, explanation and hypothesis for formulation of problem and provides relevant suggestions in the form of methods adopted, techniques tried and the comparative data for interpreting the results. It is the pre-requisite for successful conclusion the field of basic as well as social sciences.

Bulley (1971) claimed that provenance of any research requires knowledge of research studies as well as authoritative writings associated to problem under investigation, on the part of researcher. The successful completion of study and to evaluation get endangered when researcher undertakes any project without comprehensive study of its related writing. The identification of a problem, developing the design of research and determining the size and scope of a problem- all is dependent upon the care and the intensity with which research investigated the literature related to deliberate research.

In this chapter, an effort has been made to present the relevant studies which appear to have direct bearing on the present investigation. The variables involved in this study are personality characteristics and locus of control of sports-persons. The theoretical view-points of the variables under consideration have been presented in details so as to get the complete understanding of these variables and the rationale of the relationship of these variables.

2.1. PERSONALITY CHARACTERISTICS

In the field of sports psychology, the personality research was characterized by a tradition between group comparisons, e.g. athletes were compared with non-athletes, successful athletes with less successful ones, and men athletes with women athletes. Comparisons were also made among athletes representing different sports disciplines. These studies generally served performance prediction and selection goals, whether these attempts were very successful or not is difficult to say. But some studies have attempted to demonstrate an "athletic personality".

The early literature in sports personology tried to find out personality profiles which are generally associated with specific games. In late 1960's and 1970's the sprots psychologists investigated the personality trait differences between the athletes and non-athletes, successful and less successful athletes, athletes participating in individual and team games, playing one position us another and male female athletes. They were searching for accurate and definite answers to legitimate questions like "what are the truly and relatively enduring personality characteristics within traits that can have powerful effect upon how athletes perceive situation and how they act in these situations."

During the period between 1960 and 1970, more than 1000 sports personality studies were reported in various quarters of the globe but unfortunately far from consistent results and conclusions. Some reviewers of sport personality research such as Martens (1975) came to the conclusion that the general trait measures are invaluable for the purpose of prediction of appropriate sport behaviour. A contrasting viewpoint has been defended by Morgan (1980) who argues that existing research favourable to the hypothesis that traits are useful was excluded from those pessimistic reviews and he presents optimistic evidence that elite athletes display unique personality characteristics."

The research on the personality of elite performers and the prediction of success makes interesting reading, as the study in personality began with the traditional trait studies. The personality traits, both in general and in athletics context, have been subjected to investigation, assessment and analysis through the administration of the traditional self-reporting questionnaires/personality inventories (e.g. 16 PF,CPI,EPI etc.) constructed by psychologists for various purposes.

Alderman in his 1974 review of studies on sports personology commented that personality traits like sociability, dominance, extraversion, positive self-concept, emotional stability and mental toughness are consistently identified as loading on successful athletic performance. However, he further commented that the personality profiles of athletes based on measurements of the personality traits do not increase our knowledge of the dynamic tendencies which move people to action. They do not give us a picture of the 'whole' person but just segments. Little attempt has been made to show how these traits integrated with each other to cause overt behaviour. In order to rectify such inadequacies in sports personality research, attempts have been made to find out direct relationship between personality characteristics and sports performance.

Morgan has reported that his mental health model is effective in predicting success in athletes. Finding substantial empirical supports to this model, Morgan (1980) says, "An athlete who is neurotic, depressed, anxious, schizoid, introverted, confused, and fatigued and scores low on psychic vigour will tend to be unsuccessful in comparison to an athlete who is characterized by the absence of such traits." The inconclusive findings about sport personality can be traced to two major reasons; (i) "Lack of conceptual or theoretical framework" (Martens & Peterson, 1981), and (ii) "use of varied psychological tests with varied groups of subjects" (Singer, 1982). Some specific researches on which the discussion given above is based, enlisted below to have a clear idea of the samples and methodology followed by different researchers.

2.1.1. PROBLEMS IN SPORT PERSONALITY RESEARCH

The study of personality is among the most popular area in sports personology. The interest is in part attributable to the recognized importance of personality in determining the behaviour of individuals. There are some personality factors that lead to success in athletic participation. Moreover physical activity programmes are important socialization agencies that develop the personality in a desirable way.

A few questions emerge in the area of sport personality research. For example:

(i) Do various personality profiles determine the selection and success in certain sports? Or do athletes have different personality profiles than non-athletes? Do superior athletes have different personality profiles?

(ii) Does athletic participation influence the personality of the athlete? Does success or failure in sport participation influence the personality? Do specific competitive experiences produce changes in the personality of an individual?

(iii) Do female athletes differ from male athletes in personality? Are there differences in personality dispositions among athletes participation in the team as well as individual sport. Or Are there differences among athletes playing particular sports such as hockey, basketball, swimming and gymnastics?

(iv) Do individuals with high motor ability have different personality dispositions than individuals with low motor ability?

The answers to these questions have been given in the descriptions below with empirical evidences:

2.1.2 ATHLETIC PERSONALITY

An "athlete" may be any member of a team. A 'non-athlete' may be a person who has never participated in any sports activity or a person who has never played in an organized team. Many researchers have attempted to find out whether there are personality dissimilarities between so-called "athletes" and "non-athletes". Various groups of athletes have also been compared with each other as well as with non-athletes.

PERSONALITY TRAITS - ATHLETES AND NON-ATHLETES

The distinction of athletes from non athletes is made through personality differences but the particular difference yet could not be defined. After a wide research it has been concluded that there are certain personality traits which distinguish the athletes from the non-athletes or outstanding athletes from average athletes. Many investigations have tried to find personality differences between athletes and non-athletes. Currently, some sports psychologists have also been trying to differentiate between athletes and non-athletes in regard to their personality traits. In fact, the major portion of the research literature on personality structure in the field of sports psychology is related with the comparison between athletes and non-athletes (Slusher, 1964, Cooper, 1969, Sperling, 1970). Majority of the investigations have indicated that athletes differ from non-athletes on a number of personality traits.

Empirical Findings: Some Earlier Studies

In one of the earlier studies, Sperling (1942) found that more socially desirable degrees of personality development accompany a greater degree of experience in physical-education activities. He also found that athletes had higher scores on ascendance, extroversion, personal adjustment and motivation for power and less on aesthetic and theoretical values as compared to non athletes.

Heusner (1952) found some persisting personality traits in American and British Olympic champions. He found that champions were emotionally stable, dominant, venturesome, bold, uninhibited, placid, self-confident and self-assured. Weber (1953) conducted a study on 246 freshmen who were expected to take physical education at the state University of Lowa. The findings of the research declared no significant relation between total MMPI scores and fitness score. Biddulph (1954) found greater intensity of social and personal adjustment among students with higher in athletes achievement then the students ranked lower in athletic achievement.

Many studies in general tend to agree that differences do exist between athletes and non-athletes. Booth (1958) found higher degree of differences among personality of football athletes and the non athletes MMPI results declared significant difference among the athletes of various sports groups as well as non-athletes. Also an analysis of the 550 MMPI questions revealed that 22 of the items discriminated between poor and good competitors. He compared the personality traits of 145 non-athletes were compared to those of 141 athletes and higher scores for depression and anxiety were found in case of non-athletes man athletes. So he also found that differences do exist between participants in individual and team sports and also between athletes and non-athletes. Slusher (1964) examined personality characteristic difference of high school non-athletes and athletes.

He found that athletes and non-athletes differed on all the MMPI scales except the M (hypomania) and K (validity). He also found personality trait differences even within group of subjects participating in various events.

Persone (1964) revealed that difference was found among champion swimmers and the average population in 15 out of 16 factors of Cattell's 16 PF and the champion swimmers apparently possessed extreme scores on personality factors. Schendel (1965) found that the 9th grade athletes differed from the non-athletes on eight of the CPI scales, differences existed on 4 scales for the 12th grade sample and nine differences were observed for the college subjects. Hence, he supported the view that athletes and non – athletes differ in personality structure.

Kroll and Carlson (1967) contend that there is a definite personality factors existed which motivate people to select a sport and participate in it. Such factors might be different form general psychological factors relating to ordinary activity of body. Cooper (1969) lists athlete's personality structure as below:-

(i) The male competitor is basically an emotionally healthy person who tends toward extraversion.

(ii) He is self-assertive, tough-minded and self-confident with a higher capacity to reliance the stress of high level of competition.

(iii) He sets high goals for himself as well as for his team and try hard to achieve.

(iv) He has great psychological endurance and mental toughness, but a 'dominant, take charge' type of person, yet does not seek leadership.

(v) He is slightly free to express his natural aggressiveness tendencies with a high need to affiliate with others.

(vi) He is basically an orderly, organized sort of person with a lower than average tendency to act impulsively.

(vii) He will live in a socially highly desirable manner.

(viii) A superior athlete has a high need to achieve within his respective athletic endeavour.

Ogilvie (1968) also found that traits like tough-mindedness, emotional stability, consciousness, self-assuredness and outgoings consistently, self-control; low ergic tension level, were associated with athletic achievement. Malumphy (1968) used the Cattell's 16 PF to compare the personality traits of 120 women, 77 athletes and 43 non-athletes. He found athletes playing individual sport being more burnout as compared to those participating in team sports. Although the high degree of conscientiousness and tough-mindedness is found among sport participant but they were less venture some and imaginative than their counterparts i.e non sport participant.

Berger and Littlefield (1969) compared the personality of football players and non-athletes. They found insignificant differences in CPI score between outstanding football players, less outstanding athletes and non-athletes. However Cooper (1969) found differences among the non-athletes and athletes. He described and painted the picture of the athlete such as:-

(i) More venture some and socially confident;

(ii) More socially more aggressive, leading and dominant;

(iii) Having higher social adjustment, prestige, social status and self-confident;

(iv) Better competitors;

(v) Less compulsive;

(vi) Less impulsive;

(vii) Having greater tolerance for physical pain

(viii) Having lower feminine interests and higher masculine ones.

Hunt (1969) reported that Negro and white varsity athletes had similar personality profiles as did the Negro and white non-athletes. Hence, athletes, regardless of ethnic background tended to differ from the non-athletes. Studies conduced by Kane (1965), Berhram and Kroll (1967) and Dardin (1972) have indicated that determination, drive and killer instinct are the qualities that are expected to be found extraordinarily in champion athletes. They have also shown that athletes of one sport differ from those of other sport and non-athletes in their personality characteristics.

Little (1969) found that the athletic group was highly extrovert and sociable while the non-athletic group was characterized by introversion and lack of sociability. His findings were essential in agreement with those of Carmen, Zerman and Blaine (1968) and Pierce (1969) i.e. athletes display fewer neurotic symptoms than non-athletes. So, he concluded that athletes have consistently been found to differ from non-athletes on a number of personality traits. The athlete tends to be stable and extroverted with the exception of cross country runners and marathons that are characterized by introversion.

Bird (1970) examined personality differences in participants and non-participants in sports. He found that intercollegiate participants were more serious, sober, tough-minded, self-reliant, decisive, enterprising, possessing more alertness, poise when compared with the non-participants.

Sperling (1970) who used six assessment instruments to study college athletes and non-athletes, found results similar to those of Cooper (1969).Burdashaw (1971)studied personality profile of swimmers and non-swimmers among university women and found that groups did not differ significantly in the profile for 16 primary and four secondary factors. Rusch (1972) found that adult female athletes to be more reserved and tough - minded than the non-athletes.

Alderman (1974) identified sociability, dominance, extraversion, positive self-concept, mental toughness, emotional stability and conventionality as significantly discriminating personality factors of athletes as compared to non-athletes. Bhullar (1974) investigated the differences in personality adjustment of sportsmen and non-sportsmen and found marked differences in adjustment of sportsmen and non-sportswomen. A research study conducted by Kelley (1975) has shown that, as a group, the athletes exceeded the non-participants on eight CPI traits i.e. poise, ascendancy, self-assurance, dominance, sense of well being, socialization, sociability and self-acceptance. Non-participants were superior on intellectual and interest modes and femininity.

Gupta & Sharma (1976) conducted a study to determine whether differences in personality characteristics were there among athletes and non athletes. It was found that there were significant differences among all the three groups on the six variables of 16PF test. Yeater (1977) showed that a group of inter-collegiate basketball players were more tough-minded and group dependent than non-athletes. Gruber & Parkins (1978) conducted a test on 48 women major and 45 non-major women athletes who had participated in university and international meets and an equal number of non-athletes. Results indicated that women physical-education major are more happy-go-lucky than non-majors and those who competed at inter-college competitions were more sober, serious, tough minded as compared to the international participants and non-participants.

Mohan et al (1979) explored the relationship between personality and sports participation and found players to be more extrovert than non-players and had lower neuroticism indicating more stability and emotionality. Great differences were found in the personality of players and non-players. Players showed higher scores on extraversion and the non-players on neuroticism.

Later Studies in Sport Personology

Thakur and Thakur (1980) did comprehensive study of personality characteristics of the Indian college athletes and non-athlete using projective method of personality assessment and released that athletes were happier, affectionate, cardial, achievement orientry, dominant had superior capacity of organization where as the non athletes were found to be passive, rhetied exhausted with guilt and had superior imagination.

Thakur and Ojha (1981), Valliant et al (1981), Dowd and Innes (1982), Ammodt, Alexander and Kimbrough (1982) found track team members and footballers to be less patient but more dominant than the non-athlete. The findings reported by Ammodt, Alexander, & Kimbrough (1982) support these results with particular reference to baseball, football and track participations. Certain secondary traits such as extraversion (higher in athletes) do appear to distinguish athletes from non-athletes at high levels of skill (Warburton & Kane, 1966; Werner & Gottheil, 1966; Ikagami, 1970; Dishman, 1982; Freedson et al; 1983).

A comprehensive study conducted by Kaur (1984) who examined the personality profiles of track athletes, basketball, volley-ball, hockey, badminton and tennis players where they sharply differed from the non-athletes. Daino (1985) found that tennis players were more extrovert as compared to the normal population. Sharma and Shukla (1986) claimed that athletes in various sports specialties are often outgoing, emotionally stable, conscientious (rules bound), happy go lucky socially confident, self-reliant, ventures, confident, rigorous, controlled and relaxed. While the non-athletes are reserved, less intelligent, affected by feeling of weak super ego, shy, tender-mindedness, suspicious, doubting, indiscipline and tense.

Mehrabian & Bekken (1986) observed higher levels of trait dominance and trait pleasure in participants (across age and gender) in what they labelled "strenuous" sports compared with general population norms. Perhaps more meaningful is their conclusion that those who participate regularly and intensively in sports such as running, weightlifting and aerobics are healthier psychologically than the general population. Differences between athletes and non-athletes may exist in extroversion, neuroticism (lower in athletes), aggressiveness (higher in athletes), and emotional stability (Fletcher, 1971, Freedson et al 1983).

Kumar and Thakur (1986) concluded that athletes are less anxious and worrying people but have venture some personality as compared to their counterparts. These results support the findings of Eysenck et al (1982) related to less neurotic and moire extonent tendency of athletes than non athletes. Kumar & Thakur (1986) again found that athletes scored significant higher extraversion score than non-athletes, whereas non-athletes scored significantly higher neuroticism and psychoticism scores than athletes. Mohan & Kaur (1986) found in their study that the sports persons were more extrovert and less introvert than non-sportsmen. Intelligence was also found to be significantly lower for sportsmen when compared with the non-sportsmen group as a whole.

Shanker found equal stability and extravert feature in both position as well as non position winner gymnasts while studying their psychological make up. But a huge difference was found on this dimension among gymnasts and non athletes. Therefore, gymnasts have better psychological attribute for achievement in sports. Dureha (1986) compared the personality characteristics of sportspersons and non sportspersons. Significant differences in the personality characteristics of the two groups were found.

Dureha (1987) also concluded that the sportsmen and non-sportsmen differ in their personality characteristics in some factors like "emotional stability and realism about life, cheerfulness and frankness, tender-mindedness and practicability and greater control over emotion and greater regards for self-respect and social reputation."

The personality differences between athletes and non-athletes were investigated by Bhatti (1987).He concluded that both groups shared nine factors in which athletes were found to be emotionally less stable, aggressive, enthusiastic, sentimental, confident, conservative and tense as compared to non-athletes. Sahni, Sood & Mohan's (1988) research indicated that the sportsmen scored significantly higher on psychoticism as compared to non-sportsmen and the sportsmen were higher on extraversion. Mohan et al (1992) found boredom, susceptibility, venturesomeness, extraversion and psychoticism as important personality variables which can differentiate sportsmen from the non-sportsmen.

Many other investigators have also reported that athletes could be differentiated from non-athletes with respect to their self-control (Bird, 1970), self-sufficient (Ogilvie, 1968), extraversion (Peterson et al, 1967; Bushan and Aggarwal, 1978), dominance (Ammodt, et al, 1982), locus of control (Mckelvie and Hushand, 1980), death anxiety (Kumar et al, 1985), self-esteem (Kumar et al, 1985) and mental health (Kumar, et al, 1985).

With the exception of a few researchers, many huge difference among athletes and non athletes as athletes tend to be usually positive, outgoings, extrovert though socially aggressive. Such traits supports them in goal achievement and adjustment in any social situation. It is assumed that athletes have stronger drive to complete in sport and when they achieve goal, their competitive trait gets strengthened. The coaches even found task of preparing team easier when athletes have higher competitive spirit. For a coach, psychological preparation is a vital pre-requisite to be clinical preparation.

2.1.3. SEX DIFFERENCES IN PERSONALITY TRAITS OF SPORTSMEN

Effect of sex and group behaviour on personality of athletes have been revealed in a number of studies (e.g. Kane, 1964; Peterson et al 1967, Rushall, 1967; Meredith and

Harris, 1969; Foster, 1972). Kane (1964) studied the physical abilities of men and women athletes and their personality traits and concluded that both men and women athletes are highly surgent and extrovert. Though men and women both are tough minded but men are often more confident, composed and dominant. Rushall (1967) contrasted personality traits of male and female swimmers and found female swimmer more noisy, socially bold and unstrained in temperament while males were individualistic and self centered. Moreover, novice female swimmers appeared to be more introvert than female athletes of control group. (Meredith and Harris, 1969).

Considerable data has been presented regarding personality traits of female athletes. The personality structure of women athletes has been studied in the various sports such as fencing (Williams et al, 1970), basketball and golf (Johnson, 1972), lacrosse (Mushier, 1970), swimming (Ibrahim, 1967); Kane, 1966;Ogilvie, 1968); track and field (Kane, 1968) and field hockey (Acampore, 1971; Johnson, 1972). These researches compared personality traits across sports groups as well as compared team with individual sports participants. Hein, (1954); Niblock, (1960), Malumphy, (1968) studied outstanding athletes (Neal, 1963) and compared the women athletes with non-athletes. (Foster, 1969; Kane, 1966).

The results of these studies have generally shown that a few similar traits are being projected by women athletes in various sports. Women in athletic competitions appear to be more achievement–oriented (Neal; 1963; Ogilvie; 1973) tough minded (Ramsay; 1962; Malumphy; 1968; Ogilvie; 1968; Bird; 1970; Mushier; 1970); intelligent (Bird; 1970; Mushir; 1970; Johnson; 1972); creative (Bird; 1970; Mushier; 1970) aggressive (Neal; 1963; Ogilvie; 1968; Foster; 1969) dominant (Ramsay; 1962; Mushier; 1970; Ogilvie; 1968; Williams et al, 1970) and somewhat more anxious (Ramsay, 1962; Kane, 1966) as compared to intramural participants or a non-participant norm group.

Ogilvie's (1971) finding regarding the relationship between personality and athletic ability concluded that the male competitors were basically emotionally healthy persons inclined towards extraversion and were tough-minded, self-confident with a greater capacity to reliance the stress involved in high-level competition. Chadwick

(1972) found that female athletes were significantly more practical, tough-minded, group dependent, subdued and less intelligent than non-athletic females.

Gruber and Perkins (1978) found women who competed in inter-collegiate competition were significantly higher on the factors F (sober) and I (tough-minded) as compared to the non-participant group. Silva et al (1985) concluded that male athletes in general have lower neuroticism scores than would be expected in general population and their elite counterparts. Reeds (1985) indicated that there were some significant personality differences in the different grouping of athletes, i.e. male/female and team vs. individual sports participants. Male athletes showed different personality traits than female non-athletes. But, Singh, Agyajit (1986) found no sex differences in extraversion and neuroticism traits of personality in the athletic as well as hockey group.

Fraziwer (1986) compared psychological characteristics of male and female elite and non-elite marathoners. It was found that cognitive strategy of elite male marathoners was significantly different from that of non-elite marathoners. Female marathoners were found significantly higher on the measure of confusion and neuroticism-stability than male marathoners. Frank (1989) studied the psychological profiles of university athletes in developing countries. The findings supported the general consensus that male and female athletes and non-athletes possess different personality profiles. Davis (1992) found that higher emotionality appears to be characteristics of the average female athlete while normal to low emotionality is characteristic of the high performance female athletes. Kalliopuska's (1998) results show that among the top athletes men had higher score on self esteem and neuroticism than women. On the other hand, women had better self assertiveness than men.

2.1.4. PERSONALITY TRAITS OF INDIVIDUAL AND TEAM GAMES PLAYERS

Personality characteristics of athletes participating in individual and team games have also been compared. None of the personality profile could distinguish athletes and on athletes but when categorization on the basis of sport was done various differences emerged. For instance athletes who played team sports displayed (i) lesser abstract reasoning; (ii) greater extraversion; (iii) less egoistic. But the athletes who played individual sports showed: (i) higher levels of objectivity, (ii) less anxiety (iii) more dependency and (iv) lesser abstract thinking.

The results regarding differences in the personality characteristics of players of individual and team games are unequivocal. Some studies have failed to be able to find differences between team and individual athletes. (Lakie, 1962; Ikegami, 1968, Pyecha, 1970). But some studies approve of athletes in group sports being extrovert and self-confident, as compared to those participating in an individual sports who are more inclined towards introvert and stable. Kane (1967) had questioned whether a single "personality type" exists for athletes. The significant differences are seen in personality profiles of the participants where a wider range of sports are selected. There is a doubt regarding persistence of such clear cut differences the popular belief holds that the individual sport players are introvert and self-centered than their team sportsmen counterparts who are more extrovert and team oriented.

Niblock (1960) found that the individual and team sports participants scored higher on ascendancy than did non-participants. Rushall (1967) demonstrated that the male swimmers were more individualistic dominant and self-centered. Peterson, Weber & Trousdale (1967) made a comparison of personality traits of Olympic level females in the team sports and in individual sports athletes and reported that women athletes participating in individual sports were more dominant, adventurous, radical, imaginative, introvert, and forthright and were lower in sophistication than the team sport athletes. They also found team sport female athletes to be intellectually brighter and more conscientious and aggressive than the normative group of equivalent age and education. Thus, the athletes from the individual sports were more introvert, lowly sophisticated than the team sport athletes but both groups were characterized by emotional stability.

Peterson et al (1967) has also determined that women athletes who competed on individual sports scored higher on the various personality factors well dominance, adventuresome, sensitivity, introversion and self-sufficiency, but score lower on sophistication as compared to athletes who competed in the team sports. No significant difference, however, was found in the factor like sociability, intelligence, stability, suspecting nature and high sentiments.

Using 16 PFQ, Malumphy (1968) has compared the personalities of 5 groups of college women. Individual sport, team sport, subjectively judged athletes in gymnastics and synchronized swimming and non-athletes. The result showed that women who competed in team sport were more shy, anxious, introvert and possessed less leadership qualities than sports women of individual sports. Individual sports group were tough minded and possessed more tough poise and leadership asserts than the team sport groups.

Malumphy (1968) and Ogilvie (1968) conducted a related survey, where four groups of female athletes i.e. athletes in individual sports, in team sports, team-individual sports, the non-athletes and subjectively judged sports, who contrasted on various traits. The athletes of individual sports were found to be more extrovert than those from team and the team-individual groups. This findings was in opposition to the results of Peterson, Weber and Trousdale (1967). But Singer (1969) was able to distinguish team-sport athletes (baseball players) from the individual sport athletes (tennis players) in certain traits. The tennis group scored significantly higher than the baseball group on achievement, autonomy, intraception, dominance, and aggression. The baseball team scored significantly higher on the abasement factor.

Hendry (1970) reported that at the higher level of performance, team sport athletes tended to be stable-extroverts than individual sports athletes. Moore (1973) with 16 PFQ indicated that team sport group has less emotional stability, self-sufficiency and showed greater shyness and insecurity than the other group. The individual sport group displayed to be more emotionally stable and relaxed, less excitable as well as more prone towards disregarding rules than the other two groups. The combined sport group demonstrated the most serious attitude and was conscientious, persistence, tense, self-assured, self-sufficient and tough minded. Basketball players when compared to gymnasts were more self-assured and disciplined in following social rules and regulations, whereas, gymnasts happened to be more apprehensive.

King and Peter (1975) examined the relationship between personality factors and smaller segments of athletic socio-culture in a population of student athletes. The athletes were divided into team sports and individual sports. Significant differences were found among the athletes on the basis of the segments of social structure in which they participated. Many of them were related with variation in individual group orientation as well as the structure of team.

Shurr et al (1977) concluded that team sports players were more anxious, extrovert and dependent but less creative than individual sports players. But Kirkcaldy (1982) found no significant differences about the personality dimensions of team and individual players. However, Sharma and Shukla (1986) stated higher conscontinuous strength, superego outgoing, touch mindedness among individual sports athletes.

Singh, Agyajit (1986) found significant difference among the players of individual events and team games personality trait on the extraversion and neuroticism personality traits. In the case of males and females, more extrovert and neurotic trait was found among athlete group than the group of hockey players. Sandhu, Mann, Brar (1987) studied that the team players and wrestlers were equally extrovert.

2.1.5. OTHER STUDIES

Kumari Om, Kaur Jaswinder and Kamlesh (1988) undertook a study to compare personality make up of female university level players and low achievers. The study was conducted on 89 female players from different games. The game wise breakup of the sample was volleyball - 12, hockey - 19, others (Kho-Kho, Kabaddi, Gymnastics and athletics) - 12 and low achievers - 26. The age wise subjects belong to the youth group of 18-23 years. They were selected from college participants. To collect the requisite data, the Eysenck personality inventory (form A) was used. The conclusions were that volleyball players are significantly ahead of hockey players, in being stable. Hockey players, on the other hand, though significantly higher on extroversion scores, are dangerously neurotic too. Players from the other games are less extrovert and more neurotic. They do not differ with volleyball and hockey players in extroversion but they are significantly high on neuroticism in comparison to the volleyball players and significantly low in comparison to hockey players.

Charanjit Kaur (1991) conducted the study of "Motor abilities of high school children in relation to their personality traits." The study was restricted to ninth and tenth class girl students in the age range of 14 to 16 years in Patiala district. She examined 100 sports persons and 100 non sports persons. The result of this study shows that there were significant differences.

The results of Sharma (1999)'s study revealed that difference in personality pattern of players of both sex of individual and team games were not found except volleyball players. Mostly, all the male and female players were of extrovert in nature in various sports. This was also found that personality patterns of sports had not been affected by the game differences.

Reade Gregory Kenneth (1999) conducted a study on prediction of performance from selected personality traits, and State Anxiety Levels of competitive male and female gymnasts. Subjects for the study were 21 male and 35 female gymnasts, aged 9 to 23 who competed in either sectional or national qualifying meets in the United States and Canada. Path analysis, a multiple regression technique was used in the treatment of the data. Based upon the findings and within the limitations of this study, the following conclusions were drawn: (1) The personality- anxiety model was supported by explaining over 51 percent of the variability in the criterion, (2) pre-competitive anxiety was not a statistically significant prediction of gymnastics performance, (3) the hypothesis related to the personality performance relationship was not supported since the model explained only 38.1 percent of the total variability in gymnastics performance.

Kumar Kishore (1999) conducted the Achievement Motivation and Personality. A Comparative Analysis of University Volleyball and Cricket Players. The present study tries to identify the differences, if any, between achievement motivation and selected personality traits of university volley ball and cricket players. For this purpose Mangalore university volleyball (n=15) and cricket (n=16) players, who were attending final coaching camp at university campus before the inter university competitions were chosen. It should be noted here that the volleyball team secured third place at South Zone Inter University Competition and also participated in All India Inter University Competitions for the first time. The cricket team, however, lost in early - round at South Zone Inter University Competitions. Two players of the volleyball squad represented junior state and four cricket players played under 19 state zonal matches. These players were given Eysenck Personality Inventory (EPI) and Kamalesh Sports Achievement Motivation Scale (AMS) and the responses were obtained. Players with low achievement motivation (6 players) and three players had high achievement motivation. The volleyball players tended to be ambient in nature and they had moderate neurotic tendency. The cricket players, in comparison with volleyball players, did not differ much in achievement motivation and personality traits. Cricket players had moderate achievement motivation with ambient nature and had moderate neurotic tendency. Three cricket players were found to be extrovert and seven out of 16 players had neurotic tendencies.

Bhattacharjee Subhasish & Khan Babak Ali (2002) made a study on compared the psychological make up of professional physical education more students who belong to the low and higher fitness group. 120 male physical education students were selected from different physical education colleges of West Bengal for the present study. All the subjects where undergoing physical education diploma course, AAHPER Youth Fitness Test Battery was administered to assess physical fitness of all the students on the basis of their performance, the subjects were ranked from high to low in the descending order for the purpose of this study. The top and bottom twenty-seven percent were considered as the high fitness and low fitness group respectively. Cattle's 16 P.F. Questionnaire, DR VP Sharma Test Anxiety Scale. Dr. Raj Kumar Saraswat's manual for self-concept Questionnaire, Dorcan S. Butt's Sports Motivation Questionnaire were administered to assess the personality traits, level of anxiety, self-concept and sports motivation of the selected subjects respectively.

The students were categorized in high and low fitness group by using AAHPER Youth Fitness Test. The raw scores by employing Z Scale and composite score were computed. Those who scored the upper twenty seven percent, were considered as high physical fitness group and the lower twenty seven percent were considered as low physical fitness group. The score made by the students in 16 P.F. were converted into sten scores on the basis of Indian Norms available for the Questionnaire in the Anxiety scale, self concept and sports Motivation scoring was done according to the norms which described in the Manual.

Foster (2002) conducted a study to determine if 16 personality variables as measured by the Cattell's "16 PF" test could differentiate successful and less successful or outstanding athletes participating in football, basketball and baseball. The coaches of each game classified their respective players (N=483) into outstanding, successful or unsuccessful categories based on performance. Discriminate analysis of all the groups revealed on the 16 personality variables prove to be effective in differentiating successful and non-successful groups of subjects on certain personality traits.

Jaskaran Singh (2005) conducted the study: "A comparative study of personality make up of winner and non-winner sportspersons in relation to socio-economic status." The present study is aimed at exploring relationship of personality make up with winning performance in terms of their social-economic status. A sample of student sportsperson and non sportspersons was taken randomly from different colleges of Punjab, who participated in handball, cricket and athletic events at university level. The personality make up in terms of psychotocism, neuroticism and extraversion was assessed with the help of Eysenck's personality questionnaire and socio-economic status with the help of Meenakshi's socio-economic status scale. The data were analyzed following Two Way analysis of variance, with two level of winning performance i.e. winners and non winners and three levels of socio-economic status i.e. high, average and low. The results revealed that: (i) Winner and non winner sportspersons, as a whole, do not differ in their personality make up; (ii) Socio-economic status is not a significant determinant of personality make-up of Sportspersons in terms of neuroticism and extraversion, through low SES seems to enhance psychotic tendencies among sportspersons; (iii) The psychotocism among sportspersons has shown a dependence on socio economic status, where low SES acts as a catalyst to increase psychotic tendencies among non winner sportspersons.

Kabir Shah (2005) conducted the study entitled "Enhancing the personality in budding children: a development perspective" The development in early childhood is constantly changing both on the exterior and the interior, where changes are slow and gradual and they have relative effect on personality. As the body change from that of child to that of an adult, he must adopt and adjust to new concepts of what his maturing physical and mental ability to perform facilitate cognitive and the effective growth in young student and important means of both fine and gross motor skills.

There is a strong interrelationship between cognitive and motor fitness of development of body function and motor control. Through the medium of play young children develop a wide variety of locomotive, manipulative and stability ability with stable and positive self concept, the effective development that developmental experiences truly reflect children needs and interests and are within their level of ability. The sports participation has been persistently promoted as vehicle that transmits the social value of the society. The health benefit of regular physical activity and the commitments of social and psychological skill that may be learnt have been well documented

Manoj V. Hede (2005) conducted the study "India Sports Performance - Challenges in sports psychology personality and the athlete." It becomes quite obvious that participants from various athletic sub graphs differ in a number of aspects. It is commonly asserted that the football players are highly masculine and over aggressive while athletes in other sports possess other specific personality characteristics.

Ramandeep and Rathee (2006) conducted the study "Analysis of Personality differentials and achievement motivation among participants of Yoga, Athletics and Aquatics." The study was conducted to find out do inter-sports differences among the participants of yoga, athletics and aquatics on the variable of personality differentials and sports achievement motivation. An attempt was also made to find out the intra-group gender differences. Randomly 90 subjects who were participating in inter-college level competition in yoga, athletics and aquatics and both the gender groups of equal proportion were taken. Personality Inventory developed by Bhargava (1998) and Sports achievement motivation test (Kamlesh 1990) questionnaire were used. The results show that overall personality differentials were not found to be significant, similarly, the differences within male sports group and the female sports group were not found. With regard to the variable of sports achievement motivation significant differences were found between the participants of yoga, athletics and aquatics. The male participants of aquatics group were found to be significantly better than the Yoga group. Among the female sports persons, the athletes were found to be significantly better than the Yoga participants.

Gurdev Singh and Nishan Singh Deol (2009) conducted the study: "A study of personality characteristics of cyclists at various level of performance." The investigators seek to find out the differences in characteristics among cycling players at three level of performance, which would give experimental evidence to how the personality of the cycling players develop and change with the improvement in game and increase in level of performance. Randomly 90 male subjects (30 inter distt., 30 inter college and 30 inter university cyclists) of age 18 to 25 years participated in this study. Personality inventory developed by Bhargawa (1998) questionnaire was used. The interuniversity cycling riders were found to be significant better than the inter college cycling riders. The comparison of inter-college and inter district cycling riders were not found to be significant, the inter-university cycling riders were found to be significantly better than the inter district cycling riders.

Neha Garg and Kang (2009) conducted the study: "Personality profile of winner and loser of soccer players." In the present study attempt has been made to compare the personality profile of winner and loser soccer players. The study was carried on 108 subjects from various universities. 54 winner and 54 loser players were taken. Personality

NEO-FIVE FACTOR INVENTORY questionnaire was used. The present study concluded that there are significant differences between the personality of winner and losers.

Sukhvinder Singh Ghanghas and M.S. Chauhan (2009) conducted the study "A comparison of personality types of sports persons and non-sports persons." The present study focused on the personality types among sports persons and non-sports persons. One hundred sportspersons (50) and non sportsperson (50) between the age group of 17-25 years from the various colleges and M.D. University Rohtak were selected by purposive sampling. 50 sports person (25 male + 25 female) were administered Personality Inventory developed Dr. Yashbir Singh and Dr. Harmohan Singh to measure Personality Type (Extraversion-introversion). The collected data were statistically worked out and the result shows that there is no "significant difference between sports person and non-sports person in respect of personality types."

Dalbara (2012) is his study on "A comparative study of Sports Personology of Indian sportspersons at different levels of participation" found that (i) no significant differences emerged between male and female sports persons on many personality traits; except mental toughness, (ii) school levels male and females sports person did not differ on all personality traits; but college level players differed an sociability and university level players on sociability, extraversion, mental toughness and emotional maturity, (iii) sex differences between male and female non-sports persons were found in sociability, dominance and mental toughness at school level; sociability, mental toughness and emotional maturity at college level as well as combined group, (iv) significant differences were not found between sportspersons and non-sportspersons on many personality traits except emotional stability, (v) Significant differences between school and colleges level players existed on all traits of personality; whereas the college and university level players did not differ except self-concept. But school and university level players differed significantly on conventionality, mental toughness and emotional stability.

Dalbara and Agyajit (2015) in their book on "Sports Personology: A Study of Indian Sports-persons concluded that (i) no significant differences are existed between male and female sports persons on many personality traits; except mental toughness, (ii) School level male and female sport persons do not differ on all personality traits; college level players differ an sociability and university level players on sociability, extraversion, mental toughness and emotional maturity, (iii) sex differences between male and female non-sports persons are found in sociability, dominance and mental toughness at school level; sociability, mental toughness and emotional maturity at college level as well as combined group, (iv) significant differences are not found between sportspersons and non-sportspersons on many personality traits except emotional stability, (v) school level male and female players of individual games differ significant on sociability, whereas those of team games differ on mental toughness and emotional maturity. College level male or female players of individual games differ on emotional stability and team games players differ on sociability; whereas university level male and female differ on mental toughness in case of individual game and team games players differ on extraversion, mental toughness and emotional maturity, (vi) at school level, individual and team games players differ significant on sociability, dominance and self-concept. But at college and university level, individuals and team games players do not differ each other, (vii) significant differences between school and colleges level players exist on all traits of personality; whereas the college and university level players do not differ except self-concept. But school and university level players differ significantly on conventionality, mental toughness and emotional stability.

Surjit and Agyajit (2017) in their book "Psychological Characteristics of Indian Athletes: An Empirical Study" concluded that (1) athletes and non-athletes do not differ on three areas of social maturity; whether they are from school or college level, though the male athletes and non-athletes as well as female athletes and non-athletes do differ on some areas of social maturity. School and college level athletes do not differ on social maturity; though sex differences exist whether they are athletes or non-athletes. (2)

On self-efficacy, athletes and non-athletes differ, whether they are from college level or they are males or females. School and college level athletes do differ on self-efficacy and not the non-athletes. Even males and females athletes as well as non-athletes do not differ. (3) Athletes and non-athletes have the same level of self-concept; as they do not differ on all dimensions of self-concept. School and college level athletes and non-athletes do differ on some dimensions. Even males and females also differ on some dimensions of self-concept. School and college athletes also differ on some dimensions but not the males and females athletes. Even school and college non-athletes do not have any differences. But males and female non-athletes are found to have differences on many aspects of self-concept.(4) Athletes and non-athletes do not differ on many dimensions of emotional maturity. But school and college level athletes and non-athletes differ if taken separately. Male and female athletes and non-athletes do not have any differences. School and college level athletes differ on all dimensions of emotional maturity. Even male and female athletes as well as school and college non-athletes also differ; the males and females non-athletes have differences on two dimensions.

2.2. STUDIES ON LOCUS OF CONTROL

Locus of control was very largely studied in relation to social and political activities, general cognition, birth control, mutual aid, health care etc; and organized sports. Studies and theoretical literature shows that locus of control is an important psychological variable and a personality aspect which can differentiate people according to a generalized belief or expectancy attitude about control, that this expectancy can be measured and these measures are anticipative of behaviour in a variety of situations.

Rotter's social learning theory (1954, 66) is the source of the notion of LOC. The first measure of the constructs as an interpersonal variable was found by Phares (1955), and was later revised by James (1957). Other measures followed shortly thereafter (Battle and Rotter 1963; Bialer; 1961, Grave 1961; Crandall, Kathovsky and Crandall 1965; and Rotter 1966).

In the latest study on equality of educational opportunity it was indicated that locus of control was a better anticipator of behaviour than any other attitudinal, familiar school and teacher variable studied (Coleman, 1966). Reported studies on 'locus of control' have provided to be extremely useful in the prediction of a variety of behaviour. Its importance is disclosed in a variety of predictive areas including attempts in controlling the environment (Davis & Phares, 1967), risk taking (Liverant and Scodal, 1960), social effect (Ritchie & Phares, 1969), socio-cultural phenomenan (Battle and Rotter, 1963), etc. Relationship studied between locus of control and certain important social variables have no doubt contributed remarkably to its recent popularity as a research variable.

There are conflicting theoretical positions in respect to the predicted relationship between locus of control and academic achievement. The first study to relate locus of control with achievement behavior was reported by Crandall et. al. (1962). William and Stephens (1968) disclosed a negative relationship between externally and grades. Otten (1977) reported that internal LOC was remarkably related to greater academic achievement.

Stipek, Deborah, Fry, Coe and Baljal (1980) in their researches reported that internal students showed remarkably better academic achievement than externals. Kesar (1980) found that achievement of internal students did not differ significantly from the external oriented subjects.

Allen, Edward John (1982) in a research reported that internal LOC students obtained higher mathematics, reading and language scores than external students, and there is no difference found between internal and external LOC students on any achievement tests.

Callini and Kantorowski (1982) presented normative data on Rotter's Internal - External (I.E.) locus of control scale obtained from 183 female and 115 male under graduates from one same collegiate which examined that both sexes showed a trend toward greater externality over the fifteen years time between two testing. It was recommended that I.E. score may be observed as an independent variable reflecting the events and experiences of an person's life.

Chaudhary (1986) found that neuroticism was negatively correlated with internal locus of control for males and females and extraversion was positively correlated with internal LOC for both sexes only. For female, extraversion was positively correlated with internal locus of control significantly.

The results of a research by DeMan and Devies (1987) told that alienation-withdrawal due to maladjustment to society is related to low self esteem and an external LOC. Mc Ghee and Crandall (1987) found that in general, internals got better grades than externals.

Haertel, Walberg al Wang, (1990) showed that capacity of individual to overcome personal vulnerabilities and environmental adversities effectively or the ability to thrive physically and psychologically despite opposite situations.

McClelland, Robert (1991) told that gifted students in grades 6-9, found that general LOC measures did not differentiate between the groups, both scored remarkably higher on positive internal than on negative internal locus of control and there were no sex or grade effects.

Karnes & Dllio (1991) investigated 68 rural elementary gifted students, between 8 to 14 years. The scores became more internal with older ages, and the females tended to have more internal locus of control across grade 2.

Luthar (1991) finds that when persons believe that they have no power to control what happens to them, they become passive and restrictive in coping abilities. On the other hand, when people believe that situations and results are controllable, learned helplessness is avoided, and instead, active efforts are made to overcome unfavourable situations.

Long and Martinez (1994) reported differences in self-acceptance, self-esteem, masculinity, femininity and locus of control among professional female. Archer (1994) studied on 893 collegiates in Australia and said in his investigation that learning oriented students showed a much more positive attitude towards their studies and were more likely to choose a hard task to complete than their performance oriented colleagues who opted for more simple task.

Sowa, McIntyre, May and Bland (1994) described that gifted children as young as nine years have been seen to spontaneously use cognitive appraisal techniques, including problem focused techniques and emotion focused techniques (only previously seen in adults) to deal with stress.

Knight, Bruce Allen (1995) in one research of reported students investigated the gifted student's perceptions of an internal or external LOC and the influence on their behavior. Research found that gifted students who are competent academically or in other areas think that they have an internal locus of control, while underachieving gifted students perceive an external LOC.

Karnes, Frances, Mcainnis, & Christopher (1996) found self- actualization and LOC in 59 academically gifted teenagers using the reflections of self by youth and the Nowicki Strickland LOC scale for children. No significant sex or grade differences were found, though LOC scores supported the concept that high - achieving students have tendency to have more internal LOC. Dewan (1996) in her research found that criminals have higher external LOC than the non-criminals.

Hattie, Marsh, Neil and Richards; (1997) reported that at least to some extent, locus of control is a response to situations. Some psychological and educational interventions have been found to produce shifts towards internal locus of control.

Burley, Turner and Vitulli; (1999) investigated the positive relationship between learning oriented students and adaptive achievement oriented behaviours. In addition it was investigated that older students were more likely to be learning oriented but younger students more performance oriented.

Killick, Lawrence Allen (1999) had researched the relationship between sex, ethnicity and LOC among gifted teenagers. This research examined a group of 67 gifted class 8th students, 41 Asian - Canadian and 26 Caucasian, who received the intellectual achievement responsibility (IAR) questionnaire. A two factor A1 ANOVA, with sex and ethnic background as independent factors, were applied to examine the relationship between positive (7+) and negative (7-) internal LOC, sex and ethnicity. The results showed a remarkable sex X ethnicity interaction, Caucasian girls are more internal LOC orientated than Caucasian boys, where as among students of Asian descent, boys are more internal than girls. Follow - up ANOVA showed that these differences are accounted for primarily by the 7+ variables; a significant tendency was also noted for Caucasian students to score higher on 7+ and lower on 7- variables than Asian descended students.

Dole (2000) found on the research of gifted children that they show characteristics of flexibility, not all gifted children are successful and a lack of flexibility is often coupled with that lack of success. This is specifically noticeable in gifted students with learning disabilities whose traits often "include substandard self concept, substandard self efficacy, hypersensitivity, emotional ability and high levels of frustration, anxiety and self criticism."

Mamlin, Harris (2001) says that males have tendency to be more internal than females. They further found that as people get older they tend to become more internal people. Terje Manager & Ole Johan Eikeland (2001) reported that females had significantly higher internal LOC scores than boys. Boys were, however, remarkably more internally oriented than females on a subscale related to the respondents general belief in fate, while females were significantly more internally oriented than males on a school effect scale.

Prufrock Press (2004) reported 5,723 gifted teenagers. The most common personality types among gifted teenagers were those higher up in organizational structures who have tendency to be more internals, intuitive and perceiving. They have higher introversion, intuition thinking and perceiving aspects of the personality scales of the Myers-Briggs type indicator (MBTI) when compared to general high school students. Also, gifted teenagers have differences within the group by sex and ability.

Schultz and Schultz (2005) finds out remarkable differences in locus of control which have not been found for adults in a U.S. population. They further said that there may be a particular gender based differences for particular categories of items to evaluate locus of control. For example, they cite proof that males have a greater internal locus of control for questions related to academic achievement.

Michele Marie Moore (2006) described by studying achieving gifted, under achieving gifted, and non gifted students that under achieving gifted students were more externally oriented than achieving gifted students. She further found that non gifted students were more externally controlled than achieving gifted students. In regard to incompetent, men were more externally controlled than women.

Sukhdeep (2011) in her study concluded that gifted children differed with normal children on the internal and not on external locus of control; where gifted students were better on the internal locus of control than the non-gifted students. No sex differences were there on either external or internal LOC and no differences were found on both LOC between rural and urban students. She also found a positive and significant relationship between emotional intelligence and locus of control, where the internally oriented students have high emotional intelligence and externally oriented students have low E.I.

Rupinderjit (2012) in her study found that the male students were more internally oriented than the females. There was no difference on locus of control on the basis of location of schools. But the private school students have more internal LOC than govt. School students. No significant differences were found between internally and externally oriented students on all components of emotional intelligence whether they were male or female, rural or urban and govt. or private school students.

According to Ashu Jain (2012), no differences found on the internal and external locus of control of school students; on the basis of gender and types of schools; though differences exists between rural and urban school students; urban students are internally oriented and rural students are externally oriented on LOC.

The results of the research conducted by Surjit and Agyajit (2014) show that on LOC, sportspersons and non-sportspersons differed on the external and not on the internal LOC; where athletes were found to be better on external locus of control than non-sportspersons. School level sportspersons and non-sportspersons were also having differences on the external and not internal, where as college level sportspersons and non-sportspersons did not differ either on external or internal. Sportspersons of school level were better on external LOC. Moreover there were no sex differences on internal and external LOC between boys and girls students whether they were athletes or non-sportspersons.

2.3. CONCLUSION

Personality research has attracted the attention of sports psychologists, since the time this discipline came into existence. Comparison was done on the personality traits between athletes and non-athletes; men athletes with women athletes; successful athletes with less successful athletes as well as among athletes of different sports disciplines. In the early stages, more than 1000 studies were reported in the literature before 1970; though their results were inconsistent. But it was confirmed that elite athletes display unique personality characteristics.

After a great deal of research, it has been found that there are certain personality traits which distinguish the athletes from the non athletes or outstanding athletes from average athletes. Majority of the investigations have indicated that athletes differ from non-athletes on a number of personality traits. For example, champion athletes are emotionally stable, dominant, venturesome, bold, uninhibited, placid, self-confident and self-assured. They are emotionally healthy persons, extrovert, tough minded, self-assertive; have high capacity to endure of stress; set high goals, have psychological endurance and mental toughness. They are dominant, aggressive, impulsive, social and have high need to achieve and have greater tolerance for physical pain. They are more conscientious, have good self-concept, conventionality and are happy go lucky person.

With the exception of a few researchers, many have found that sportspersons differ from non- sportspersons. It seems the sportspersons' traits are usually positive. For example, sportspersons have been explained as extrovert, easy going, and socially aggressive. These are positive features that would probably beneficial sportspersons in any social situation. It is normally accepted as fact that players are highly competitive it is concluded that an individual need to have a strong competitive drive to participate in sport. After all, competition is the basic nature of the game. When sportspersons compete successfully, the competitive characteristic seems to be strengthened. Trainers who train highly competitive sportspersons will have an easier job in preparing the team for an opponent, as more time can be devoted to technical training than to motivation. For the trainer, psychological training should equally competent as technical preparation.

CHAPTER III

METHOD AND PROCEDURE

Research is purposive, scientific and systematic consideration. It requires a person to proceed in a definite direction along with properly defined methodology. Methodology makes the most important input into the enhancement of any research. To undertake any research, it is necessary to design and plan the procedure and the strategy of inquiry. A lot of methods and means are applied in research but it is the characteristics of the problem under consideration which decides the adaptation of a specific method and procedure. A procedure to the researcher is as tools to the carpenters. If a scholar cannot clearly describe his methods, the chances are that it is too indefinite and general to give sufficiently good results.

3.1. DESIGN OF THE STUDY

In this research, descriptive and survey method was applied. To evaluate two variables of the research, two different standardized tests were administered to the sports-persons of inter-college and inter-university levels of competition. Here personality characteristics and locus of control were dependent variable and (ii type of the competition, i.e.; inter-college and inter-university levels competitions and (iii) type of the games i.e.; ball games and combat sports were the independent variables.

3.2. SAMPLE

In order to achieve the objectives and test the hypotheses :a sample of 600 female sports-persons was selected, out of which 300 were from inter-college level and 300 were from inter-university level competition. An attempt was made to have 50% of the sample from the ball games and 50% players from the combat sports. The players of the ball games were selected from Baseball, Football and Handball and players of the combat sports were taken from the Judo, Taekwondo and Wrestling. The number of players belonging to six games of different colleges has been differentiated.

The sample size is depicted graphically in the following figure:

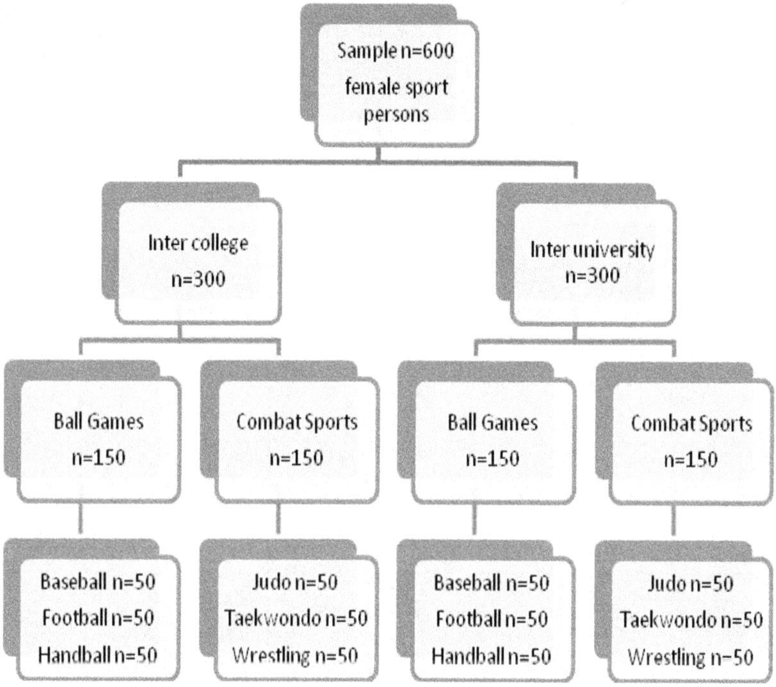

The distribution of the sample is given below.

3.1 INTER-COLLEGE LEVEL COMPETITION

Name of the college	Baseball	Football	Handball	Judo	Taekwondo	Wrestling
1. K.C.W. Ludhiana	16		02	07		07
2. G.N.G College Ludhiana				07	05	
3. G.N.Kh. College for women Ludhiana	16			07	07	
4. R.G.C. Ludhiana	16	20	16	06	07	05
5. Panjab University campus, Chandigarh	02					
6. G.H.G Kh. college Sadhar		20	16			07
7. Khalsa College Mahilpur		10				07
8. M.C.M D.A.V. College Chandigarh			16	07	07	
9. G.N. College, Narangwal				05		05
10.G.C.G. Ludhiana				06	07	07
11.D.A.V. College, Hoshiarpur				05	06	
12.S.G.G.S. Kh. College for women Chandigarh						06
13.Dev Samaj college Ferozepur						06
14. S.D.P. College for women Luduiana					05	
15. Arya College for Women Ludhiana					06	
Total	**50**	**50**	**50**	**50**	**50**	**50**

3.2 INTER-UNIVERSITY LEVEL COMPETITION

Name of the university	Baseball	Football	Handball	Judo	Taekwondo	Wrestling
Panjab University Chandigarh	20	16	14	10	12	10
Pbi. University Patiala	20	16	12	10	12	12
G.N.D. U. Amritsar	10	08	14	12	08	10
Delhi University		10				
L.P.U. Jalandhar			10	10	10	
K.U. Kurukshetra				08		10
J.N. University Delhi					08	
P.A.U. Ludhiana						08
Total	**50**	**50**	**50**	**50**	**50**	**50**

3.3. TESTS/TOOLS USED

All the sportspersons were administered the following two standardized tests for measuring their psychological characteristics.

1. **Sports Specific Personality Test:-** For the measurement of personality traits of sportspersons; Specific Sports Personality Test devised by Cheema and Singh (2005) was administered in Punjabi\English version to all the subjects of the study; i.e. females. This test has 100 items which measure seven personality traits. It is a reliable and valid test.

2. **Locus of control Test: -** To measure the locus of control trait (i.e internal and external) of the sportspersons; the scale of Dr. N. Hasnain and Dr. D.D Joshi (1992) was administered in Punjabi/Hindi medium to all the players of the study i.e females. This questionnaire has 36 items which measure internal and external LOC.

3.4 DESCRIPTION OF THE TESTS

1. **SPORTS-SPECIFIC PERSONALITY TEST: -** This questionnaire has 100 items and measures seven of personality traits for Dominance, sociability, conventionality, extraversion, self-concept, mental toughness and emotional stability.

2. **SCORING PROCEDURE**

The test is scored as such:

	Positive Items	Negative items
Never	1	4
Sometimes	2	3
Often	3	2
Always	4	1

The following is the sequence of the items in each dimension of the personality test.

1.	Sociability	Positive	1, 8,15, 22, 36, 57, 64, 71, 85, 92, 99	= 11
		Negative	29, 43, 50, 78.	= 4
2.	Dominance	Positive	2,9,23,30,37,44,51,,72,79,93	=10
		Negative	16,58, 65, 86,100	= 5
3.	Extraversion	Positive	10,17,24,31,38,66,73,80	= 8
		Negative	3, 45, 52,59, 87	= 5
4.	Conventionality	Positive	4, 11, 18, 32, 39, 53, 74, 81, 88	= 9
		Negative	25, 46, 60, 67	= 4
5.	Self-Concept:	Positive	12,19,26,33,40,61,68,82,89,96	=10
		Negative	5, 47, 54, 75	= 4
6.	Mental Toughness	Positive	6, 13, 20, 34, 69,83,90,95	= 8
		Negative	27,41,48,55,62,76,97	= 7
7.	Emotional Stability	Positive	7,14,21,28,35,42,49,56,77,84,91,94	=12
		Negative	63, 70, 98	= 3

Reliability of the Test

For test-retest, reliability of both the medium of test was found out by conducting the test of female players after a gap of 15 days and co-efficient of correlation were worked out between the scores of the first administration of the test and the second administration of the test for the entire test and for sub-tests. The correlation co-efficient of the scores of the first and the second administration of the English medium of the test were found out which was 0.90, 0.84, 0.69, 0.93, 0.82, 0.87, 0.58 and 0.86 for dominance, sociability, conventionality, extraversion, self-concept, mental toughness and emotional stability and the entire test respectively. The corresponding values for the Punjabi medium of the test were 0.93, 0.84, 0.68, 0.91, 0.81, 0.85, 0.57 and 0.85 respectively. To check the internal consistency the inter correlation between seven sub tests each representing one dimension was calculated and their correlation with the entire test was also found.

The split half procedure was also applied for the Sports Specific Personality test in this study. The values got to be 0.86, 0.77, 0.61, 0.82, 0.80, 0.92, 0.62 and 0.91 respectively for Punjabi medium, whereas the respective values of reliability co-efficients for English medium of the test got to be 0.86, 0.76, 0.61, 0.81, 0.78, 0.90, 0.61 and 0.90 respectively. It means that reliability of both the mediums of the test on the basis of the test-retest procedure and split half procedure was got to be quite high and we can say that the test is quite reliable.

Validity of the Test

The content and construct validity was got with the help of expert view point and concurrent validity was found by correlating scores obtained by conducting the test to the players and aggregate rating scores of the 10 trainers awarded to players. It was found because first question in validation is whether the new test agrees with the present source of information. The rating scores of the trainers were taken on a four point scale, i.e;

1. Very much true
2. true
3. true to some extent and
4. Not true

after describing clearly the each characteristic to them. The scores so obtained were correlated with the scores obtained earlier by conducting the test to 80 subjects.

Correlation values were got between test scores and rating scores awarded by trainers found to be 0.66, 0.63, 0.62, 0.56, 0.61, 0.53, 0.62, 0.64 respectively in case of dominance, sociability, conventionality, extraversion, self-concept, mental toughness and emotional stability and total test which is again quite high and we can say that the test is quite valid as it measures what it is supposed to measure.

2. LOCUS OF CONTROL SCALE (1992)

Locus of control scale by Dr. Hasnain N and Dr. D.D. Joshi is known as a tool that measures the locus of control of players. The scale evaluates the internal and external LOC of the player. This scale is favoured over others in modern research because:

a) Rotter's (propounded the concept of LOC) genuine I.E. questionnaire is based and prepared in the different Socio-Cultural situations than Indian-ones.

b) The existing questionnaire was prepared and standardized to impart a simple scale to Indian researchers.

c) This is simple to administer.

d) Its scoring is simple and interpretation is also not difficult.

The questionnaire consists of 36 items of 16 positive items (1, 3, 6, 7, 9, 13, 15, 16, 18, 23, 26, 27, 29, 30, 34 and 35) that measure internal LOC and 20 negative items (2, 4, 5, 8, 10, 11, 12, 14, 17, 19, 20, 21, 22, 24, 25, 28, 31, 32, 33 and 36) which measures external L.O.C.

SCORING

The existing questionnaire is a three point scale. The subjects have to respond in terms of 'Always' 'sometimes' and 'Never' and the scores of 2, 1 and 0 are given to the positive (16) items for 'Always', 'Sometimes', and 'Never' respectively. The scoring on negative items is done in a reverse order. The high level score on the scale is 72 and the low level is 0. The positive items are related to internal L.O.C. and the negative items with external LOC., so the higher the score in the questionnaire, the more internally oriented the person will be and the low shows that the players will be externally oriented.

RELIABILITY AND VALIDITY OF THE SCALE:-

Coefficient of reliability was calculated using the following methods:-

1) **Internal consistency**. The internal consistency coefficient of reliability was determined by even-odd procedure (N=50) using spearman-Brown prophecy formula. The reliability coefficient thus calculated was got to be 0.55.

2) **Temporal Stability**. Test-retest (N=50) method for the reliability coefficient of temporal stability after a gap of 14 days was got to be 0.76.

VALIDITY: The validity of the questionnaire was got by calculating the coefficient of correlation (N=50) between the scores of players on this scale and on Roma Pal's (1983) scale. The coefficient of correlation thus calculated came to be 0.76. Moreover critical Ratio between the means of inter college females (N=300) and inter university (N=300) was found to be 5.87 which was significant beyond 0.01 level of significance. The means of inter college and inter university females were found to be 20.83 and 19.23 respectively. Thus the inter college females were significantly more internally oriented than inter university females.

3.5. PROCEDURE FOR DATA COLLECTION

In the beginning of data collection the researcher met the players of inter college and inter university level, from where she intended to collect the data. She explained the design and objectives of her research project and asked for their co-operation and help in collecting the data. After the sports-persons were got seated comfortably and explained regarding the task which they were expected to perform. They were ensured to them that it was merely a research work and that it would not affect their sports performance. Moreover the results and scores of the test would not be revealed to anybody except themselves if they were interested. The same would be kept confidential and used for research purpose only.

After assuring the anonymity, they were given copies of the test booklets along with the response sheet. They were given instructions on how to complete the tests. They were directed to be honest in their responses and not to divulge anything to any other players and they should not try to consult each other while giving the responses. They were given free time to complete the whole test. The students took about 40-50 minutes to give answers to all the statements. Then the response sheets were collected from them and if any response sheet was left incomplete; the player was asked to complete it.

3.6. PROCEDURE AND STATISTICAL TECHNIQUES

When the data was collected, the response sheets of these two tests were scored on the basis of scoring keys given in their respective manuals. The raw scores were statistically analysed. The following statistical techniques had been applied on the raw data in order to find out the results:

(i) The mean, SD, and SE of the scores of all the variables related to different groups were calculated,

(ii) t-ratios were found out in order to know the significant differences on scores of seven traits of personality and two dimensions of locus of control between two groups formed on the basis of types of games, i.e. female sportspersons of ball games and combat sports.

(iii) One way ANOVA was applied to know the significant differences on the scores of seven traits of personality and two dimensions of locus of control among the female athletes of six games on the basis of levels of competition, i.e.; inter-college and inter-university level.

(iv) Pearson's product moment of correlation was worked out to find the relationships between two variables as well as inter-co-relationship among all these variables under study.

(v) Post-hoc ANOVA was used where it was applicable.

These results were explained and discussed by drawing out the tables and graphs. Researches were measured on the basis of the past researches already conducted and accessible in the literature. Conclusions were prepared and suggestions were given to prepare the policies for sports programming of sports-persons.

CHAPTER IV

ANALYSIS OF DATA, INTERPRETATION OF RESULTS AND DISCUSSION

The present investigation was concerned with the selected psychological characteristics of sports-persons at different level of participation. For this purpose, psychological characteristics like Sociability, Dominance, Extraversion, Conventionality, Self-Concept, Mental Toughness and Emotional Stability along with External and Internal locus of control were studied for 600 female sports-persons who had participated at Inter-College and Inter-University level of competition. In order to measure psychological characteristics of the female sports-persons, two standardized inventories were administered to them, i.e. Sports Specific personality Inventory devised by Singh & Cheema (2005) and Locus of Control Inventory by Hasnain and Joshi (1992). The sports-persons belonged to ball-games like Football, Baseball and Handball; which were also the team games whereas sports-persons from Combat Sports were from Judo, Taekwondo and Wrestling which were also the individual games.

4.1. Descriptive Statistics of Personality Characteristics

After the data collection, the response sheets of all the subjects of the study were scored on the basis of the scoring keys as provided in their respective manuals. The raw scores were statistically analyzed with the help of SPSS software program of the computer system. The main objective of the present study was to measure the personality traits like Sociability, Dominance, Extraversion, Self-Concept, Conventionality, Mental Toughness and Emotional Stability as well as External and Internal locus of control of the female athletes who have participated at Inter-College and Inter-University level. In order to achieve this objective, descriptive statistics were computed like mean, median mode, standard deviation, skewness and kurtosis etc which are given in the following tables.

Table 4.1 describes the mean, median, mode, standard deviation, skewness and kurtosis of scores of all the seven characteristics of personality as well as Internal and External locus of control variables.

Table 4.1. Descriptive Statistics of Personality Characteristics of All Sportspersons.

Descriptive Statistics	Sociability	Dominance	Extraversion	Conventionality	Self Concept	Mental Toughness	Emotional Stability	Internal LOC	External LOC
N	600	600	600	600	600	600	600	600	600
Mean	43.0	40.80	35.88	35.54	38.92	40.21	40.75	9.67	23.5
Median	42.0	41.0	36.00	36.00	39.00	40.00	41.00	9.50	23.0
Mode	41.0	41.00	36.00	37.00	42.00	40.00	37.00	5.00	20.0
Std. Deviation	5.85	4.23	5.03	4.30	5.10	4.60	5.18	4.75	6.48
Skewness	0.19	-0.12	0.16	-0.04	0.09	0.15	0.17	0.28	-0.06
Kurtosis	-0.09	0.07	0.14	-0.08	0.00	0.69	0.67	-0.46	-0.20

As per the table 4.1, mean scores and SDs for seven personality traits were 43.07±5.85, 40.80±4.23, 35.88±5.03, 35.54±4.30, 38.92±5.10, 40.21±4.60 and 40.75±5.18 for Sociability, Dominance, Extraversion, Conventionality, Self-Concept, Mental Toughness and Emotional Stability. And the same for Internal and External locus of control were 9.67±4.75 and 23.52±6.48 respectively. The median and mode values stands contrast to each other to 42.00 & 41.00; 41.00 & 41.00; 36.00 & 36.00; 36.00 & 37.00; 39.00 & 42.00; 40.00 & 40.00 and 41.00 & 37.00 respectively, whereas for Internal and External locus of control, the same values were 9.50 & 5.00 and 23.00 & 20.00 .All these values show that the data have a normal distribution, as the values of mean and median are closer to each other and there is a less deviation. Even the norms as given in the manual of the original test devised by Singh & Cheema (2005) reveals that the mean and standard values of this research study were quite close to the values as given in the test.

Skewness and kurtosis had also been found out to know if the data falls on the normal distribution or not. If not so, then how much divergence from normality is present. When a distribution of scores is not symmetrical, it is said to be asymmetrical or skewed. Skewness is the measure of the degree of its departure from symmetry. The frequency distribution of a set of scores is called symmetrical about its mean if the number of frequency at any point on the upper side of the mean is exactly the same to the number of frequency at an equidistant point on the lower side of mean. It has been observed that skewness on all the personality characteristics ranged between -0.04 to 0.28. A normal curve has S_k=0. Deviation from normality can be in negative and positive direction leading to negatively skewed and positively skewed distribution respectively. So it can be said that the data fell on the normal distribution.

The kurtosis of a distribution refers to its curvedness or peakedness. The peakedness is based on the degree of concentration of the scores near the central tendency. A normal distribution has Ku=0.263. If Ku is less than 0.263, the distribution is leptokurtic and if ku is greater than 0.263, the distribution is platykurtic. A distribution having a high concentration of scores near the central tendency and high tails as compared to a normal distribution with the same standard deviation is called leptokurtic; whereas distribution having low concentration of scores in the neighbourhood of the central tendency and low tails as compared to a normal distribution with the same standard deviation is called platykurtic.

In the present study, Ku ranged between -0.08 to 0.69. Only in the case of Mental Toughness and Emotional Stability, the same were 0.69 and 0.67, whereas in all other characteristics, Ku values were less than 0.263. So it can be said that data had normal distribution. As the measures of central tendencies, i.e.; mean median and mode clustered around nearer scores, it can be inferred that the distributions in all these personality traits were almost normal, as in most of the cases, the index of kurtosis was lower than o.263, the score of peakedness of a normal distribution.

Table 4.2 shows the descriptive statistics of all seven personality characteristics as well as Internal and External locus of control of female sport-persons who participated at Inter-College level competition, i.e. mean, median, mode, SDs, skewness and kurtosis etc. All these values can easily be compared with those of the total sample.

Table 4.2. Descriptive Statistics of Personality Characteristics of Female Sports-Persons of Inter College Level.

Descriptive Statistics	Sociability	Dominance	Extraversion	Conventionality	Self Concept	Mental Toughness	Emotional Stability	Internal LOC	External LOC
N	300	300	300	300	300	300	300	300	300
Mean	43.28	40.86	36.04	35.37	38.76	40.58	41.03	9.42	24.43
Median	43.00	41.00	36.00	36.00	38.50	40.00	41.00	9.00	24.00
Mode	41.00	41.00	36.00	37.00	36.00	39.00	41.00	5.00	20.00
Std. Deviation	6.34	4.37	5.36	4.50	5.37	5.01	5.45	4.98	7.03
Skewness	0.13	-0.09	0.02	-0.07	0.05	0.00	0.02	0.50	-0.02
Kurtosis	0.05	0.14	0.26	-0.09	0.00	0.83	0.89	-0.31	-0.52

As per the above table, the mean scores were 35.37 in case of Conventionality and 43.28 of Sociability which are nearer to the mean of the total sample and their median values were very closer to the mean scores which show that the data was normally distributed. All the skewness indexes were also nearer to 0 and kurtosis index was also less than 0.263 except in the case of Mental Toughness and Emotional Stability which again prove that distribution of the scores fell on normality.

Table 4.3 shows the descriptive statistics of all seven personality characteristics as well as Internal and External locus of control of female sport-persons who participated at Inter University level competition, i.e. mean, median, mode, SDs, skewness and kurtosis etc. All these values can easily be compared with those of the total sample.

TABLE 4.3 Descriptive Statistics of Personality Characteristics of Female Sports-Persons of Inter University Level

Descriptive Statistics	Sociability	Dominance	Extraversion	Conventionality	Self Concept	Mental Toughness	Emotional Stability	Internal LOC	External LOC
N	300	300	300	300	300	300	300	300	300
Mean	42.86	40.74	35.72	35.71	39.09	39.84	40.48	9.92	22.61
Median	42.00	41.00	35.00	35.00	39.00	40.00	40.00	10.00	23.00
Mode	42.00	41.00	34.00	34.00	40.00	38.00	39.00	12.00	23.00
Std. Deviation	5.33	4.10	4.67	4.08	4.83	4.12	4.90	4.49	5.76
Skewness	0.25	-0.18	0.35	0.03	0.17	0.29	0.34	0.02	-0.36
Kurtosis	-0.59	-0.04	-0.15	-0.13	-0.08	0.12	0.34	-0.58	-0.04

As per the above table, it was found that in case of the Inter University level, the mean scores of the female sportspersons were similar to their counterparts of the Inter-College level competition. The mean and median scores indicate that they were very closer to each other and hence there were less deviations in their scores. The skewness and kurtosis indexes also reveal that the data was normally distributed.

4.2 COMPARISON BETWEEN INTER-COLLEGE AND INTER-UNIVERSITY LEVEL FEMALE SPORTS-PERSONS ON PERSONALITY CHARACTERISTICS

One of the objectives of the study was to make comparison between female sport-persons of Inter-College and Inter-University level competition on personality characteristics like Sociability, Dominance, Extraversion, Self-Concept, Conventionality, Mental Toughness and Stability as well as Internal and External locus of control. For this purpose, mean scores, standard deviations and standard errors of the scores for all the personality characteristics were calculated for the Inter-College and Inter-University level female sports-persons and then their t-ratios were computed in order to find out if significant differences existed and if so, at what level of significance. These results have been presented in the following tables.

Table 4.4 gives the mean score differences on all the seven personality characteristics as well as Internal and External locus of control between the female sport-persons of Inter-College and Inter-University level competition. t-values shows whether the differences are significant or not and if so, at what level of significance.

Table 4.4 Mean, SD and t-values of personality characteristics Between Inter-College and Inter-University level sport-persons

Variables / Institute		N	Mean	SD	SE_B	t-value	df	p-value
Sociability	College	300	43.28	6.34	0.37	0.885	598	0.376
	University	300	42.86	5.33	0.31			
Dominance	College	300	40.86	4.37	0.25	0.347	598	0.729
	University	300	40.74	4.10	0.24			
Extraversion	College	300	36.04	5.36	0.31	0.763	598	0.446
	University	300	35.72	4.67	0.27			
Conventionality	College	300	35.37	4.50	0.26	0.978	598	0.328
	University	300	35.71	4.08	0.24			
Self Concept	College	300	38.76	5.37	0.31	0.800	598	0.424
	University	300	39.09	4.83	0.28			
Mental Toughness	College	300	40.58	5.01	0.29	1.976*	598	0.049*
	University	300	39.84	4.12	0.24			
Emotional Stability	College	300	41.03	5.45	0.31	1.292	598	0.197
	University	300	40.48	4.90	0.28			
Internal LOC	College	300	9.42	4.98	0.29	1.291	598	0.197
	University	300	9.92	4.49	0.26			
External LOC	College	300	24.43	7.03	0.41	3.457**	598	0.001**
	University	300	22.61	5.76	0.33			

*Significant at 0.05 level (t should be between 1.96 and 2.58)
**Significant at 0.01 level (t should be more than 2.58)

As per the table 4.4, no significant differences were found between Inter-College and Inter-University level female sports-persons on almost all the personality characteristics except Mental Toughness and External locus of control variables. In case of Mental Toughness, t-value was found to be 1.976 which is significant at 0.05 level and in case of External locus of control, the same was 3.457 which is significant at 0.01 level. Their mean scores indicate that college level sportspersons were having high Mental Toughness (M=40.58) as compared their university level counterparts (M=39.84). Similarly college level female players were more Externally oriented (M=24.43) than university level players (M=22.61) In all other personality characteristics they stood at the same level, as no significant differences were found out.

The mean scores of all personality characteristics of Inter-College and Inter-University level female sports-persons have been depicted graphically through histogram shown in the Figure 4.1

Figure 4.1 Histogram showing the mean scores of all personality characteristics of Inter-College and Inter-University female sports-persons

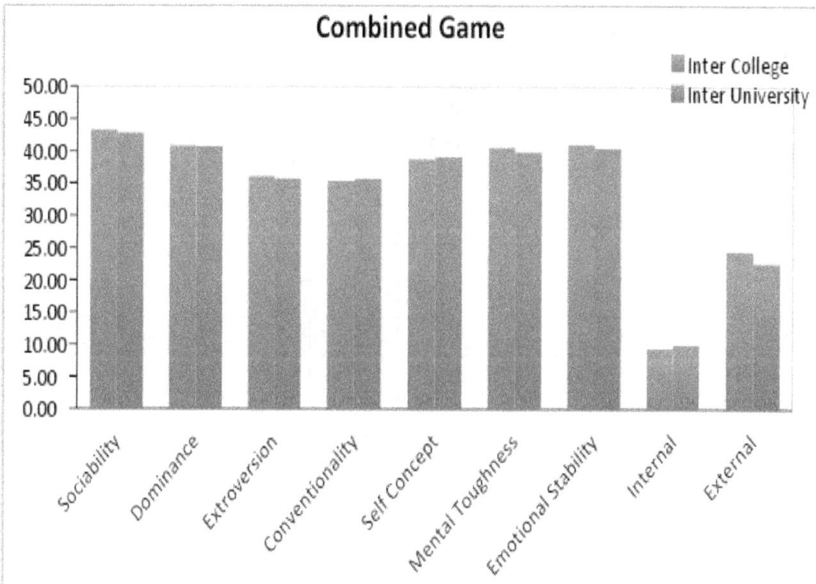

An attempt was made to find out the significant differences on all the personality characteristics between the female sport-persons of Inter-College and Inter-University level competition by taking each game separately. Mean and standard deviation scores of all the personality characteristics were calculated and then t-ratios were computed for all the six games separately, e.g. Baseball, Football, Handball, Judo, Taekwondo and Wrestling.

Table 4.5 shows the mean scores differences on all these seven personality characteristics as well as Internal and External locus of control between the female sport-persons of Baseball game participating at Inter-College and Inter-University level competition.

Table 4.5 Mean, SD and t-ratios of personality characteristics of female Baseball players of inter college and inter university level competition

Variables	Institute	N	Mean	SDs	SE$_M$	t-value	df	p-value
Sociability	College	50	42.98	5.22	0.74	0.216	98	0.829
	University	50	42.74	5.87	0.83			
Dominance	College	50	40.90	5.09	0.72	0.251	98	0.802
	University	50	40.66	4.44	0.63			
Extraversion	College	50	36.26	5.20	0.74	1.450	98	0.150
	University	50	34.76	5.15	0.73			
Conventionality	College	50	36.02	4.03	0.57	0.799	98	0.426
	University	50	35.34	4.47	0.63			
Self Concept	College	50	39.32	4.83	0.68	0.261	98	0.794
	University	50	39.58	5.11	0.72			
Mental Toughness	College	50	40.66	5.15	0.73	1.627	98	0.107
	University	50	39.10	4.41	0.62			
Emotional Stability	College	50	41.72	5.06	0.72	1.365	98	0.176
	University	50	40.32	5.20	0.73			
Internal LOC	College	50	9.02	4.53	0.64	1.588	98	0.116
	University	50	10.42	4.28	0.61			
External LOC	College	50	22.14	5.85	0.83	1.192	98	0.236
	University	50	23.42	4.84	0.69			

As per the table 4.4, no significant differences were observed on all the personality characteristics between the female players of Baseball game participating at

Inter-College and Inter-University level, as all these t-values were found out to be non significant. It means that the college and university level players were at the same level on all these seven personality characteristics as well as Internal and External locus of control.

The mean scores of all personality characteristics of Inter-College and Inter-University level female sports-persons of Baseball game have been depicted graphically through histogram in the Figure 4.2.

Figure 4.2 Histogram showing the mean scores of all personality characteristics of Inter-College and Inter-University female sports-persons of Baseball game

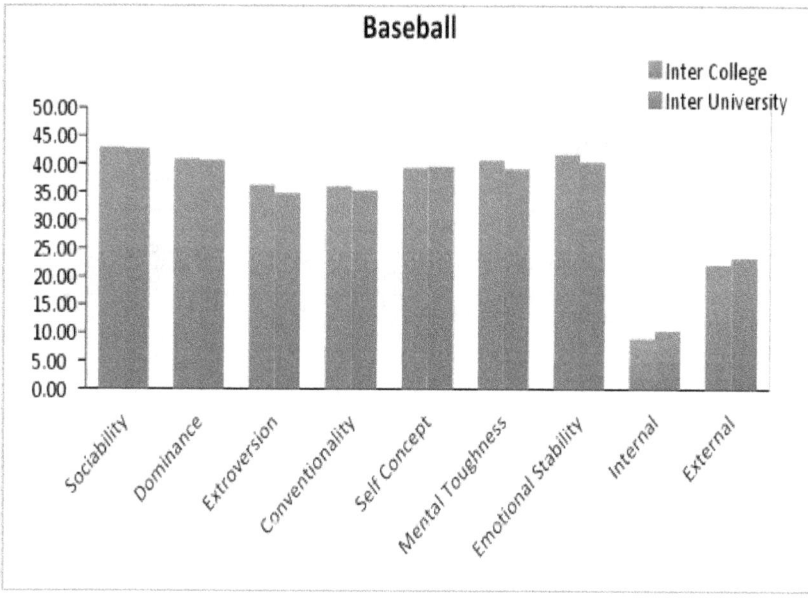

Table 4.6 shows the mean scores differences on all these seven personality characteristics as well as Internal and External locus of control between the female sport-persons of Football game participating at Inter-College and Inter-University level competition.

Table 4.6 Mean, SD and t-ratios of personality characteristics of female Football players of inter college and inter university level competition

Variables	Institute	N	Mean	SDs	SE	t-value	df	p-value
Sociability	College	50	42.24	6.97	0.99	1.793	98	0.076
	University	50	44.54	5.80	0.82			
Dominance	College	50	39.38	5.32	0.75	1.626	98	0.107
	University	50	40.98	4.48	0.63			
Extraversion	College	50	35.12	6.22	0.88	1.649	98	0.102
	University	50	36.96	4.86	0.69			
Conventionality	College	50	34.24	4.68	0.66	2.567*	98	0.012*
	University	50	36.58	4.43	0.63			
Self Concept	College	50	37.24	6.36	0.90	1.979*	98	0.051
	University	50	39.48	4.85	0.69			
Mental Toughness	College	50	39.84	6.40	0.91	0.492	98	0.624
	University	50	40.38	4.38	0.62			
Emotional Stability	College	50	39.32	5.96	0.84	1.256	98	0.212
	University	50	40.70	4.98	0.70			
Internal LOC	College	50	8.46	4.38	0.62	1.260	98	0.211
	University	50	9.70	5.41	0.76			
External LOC	College	50	32.52	5.89	0.83	9.409*	98	0.0001*
	University	50	21.50	5.82	0.82			

*Significant at 0.05 level (t should be between 1.96 and 2.58)
** Significant at 0.01 level (t should be more than 2.58)

As per the table 4.6, significant differences were evinced in case of Conventionality (t= 2.56, $p<0.012$), Self-Concept (t=1.979, $p<0.051$) and External locus of control (t=9.409, p<0.001) between Football female sports-persons participating at Inter-College and Inter-University level competition but not on all other personality characteristics, as all other t-values were found to be non significant. In case of Conventionality and Self-Concept variables, university level players were better (M=36.58 & 39.48) as compared to college level players (M=34.24 & 37.24). But in case of External LOC, College level players were found to have higher mean of 32.52 than the university level players where mean is 21.50.

The mean scores of all personality characteristics of Inter-College and Inter-University level female sports-persons of Football game have been depicted graphically through histogram given in the Figure 4.3

Figure 4.3 Histogram showing the mean scores of all personality characteristics of Inter-College and Inter-University female sports-persons of Football game

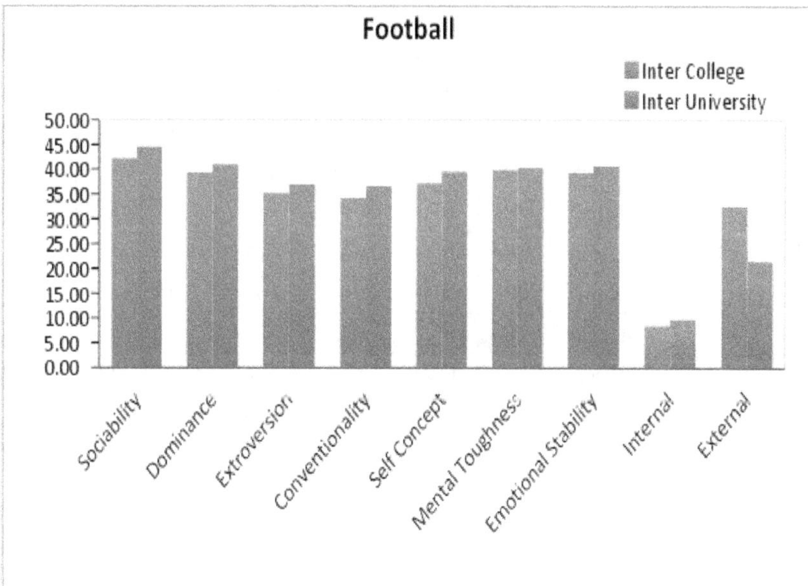

Table 4.7 shows the mean scores differences on all these seven personality characteristics as well as Internal and External locus of control between the female sport-persons of Handball game participating at Inter-College and Inter-University level competition.

Table 4.7 Mean, SD and t-ratios of Personality Characteristics of female Handball players of inter college and inter university level competition

Variables	Institute	N	Mean	SDs	SE_D	t-value	df	p-value
Sociability	College	50	40.36	5.32	0.75	4.32**	98	0.000**
	University	50	44.66	4.61	0.65			
Dominance	College	50	39.46	3.41	0.48	2.398*	98	0.018*
	University	50	41.12	3.51	0.50			
Extraversion	College	50	33.96	4.74	0.67	3.23**	98	0.002**
	University	50	37.02	4.71	0.67			
Conventionality	College	50	33.62	3.93	0.56	3.86**	98	0.000**
	University	50	36.68	3.98	0.56			
Self Concept	College	50	36.72	5.21	0.74	3.45**	98	0.001**
	University	50	40.16	4.74	0.67			
Mental Toughness	College	50	39.56	4.73	0.67	2.393*	98	0.019*
	University	50	41.72	4.28	0.61			
Emotional Stability	College	50	38.94	5.40	0.76	1.609	98	0.111
	University	50	40.74	5.78	0.82			
Internal LOC	College	50	13.24	4.63	0.66	4.75**	98	0.000**
	University	50	8.74	4.84	0.68			
External LOC	College	50	22.50	5.40	0.76	3.17**	98	0.002**
	University	50	18.72	6.45	0.91			

*Significant at 0.05 level (t should be between 1.96 and 2.58)
** Significant at 0.01 level (t should be more than 2.58)

As per the above table, differences on many personality characteristics were found to be significant between university level and college level female sports-persons of Handball game, e.g. Sociability ($t= 4.321, p<0.001$), Dominance ($t=2.398, p<0.018$),

Extraversion (t=3.237, p<0.002), Conventionality (t=3.869, p<0.001), Self-Concept (t=3.454, p<0.001), Mental Toughness (t=2.393 , p< 0.019), Internal LOC (t= 4.75 , p<0.001), and External LOC (t= 3.177, p< 0.002), but not in the case of Emotional Stability, where t-value of 1.609 was not statistically significant. The mean scores indicate that university level female players of Handball game were having high mean scores on Sociability (M=44.66), Dominance (M=41.12), Extraversion (M=37.02), Conventionality(M= 36.68), Self-Concept (M=40.16), Mental Toughness (M=41.72) than the college level players whose mean scores can be compared as 40.36, 39.46, 33.96, 33.62, 36.72, & 39.56 respectively. On the other hand, college level players were better on both Internal and External locus of control as their mean score were 13.24 and 22.50 as compared to their university counterparts (M= 8.74 and 18.72).

The mean scores of all personality characteristics of Inter-College and Inter-University level female sports-persons of Handball game have been depicted graphically through histogram given in the Figure 4.4

Figure 4.4 Histogram showing the mean scores of all personality characteristics of Inter-College and Inter-University female sports-persons of Handball game

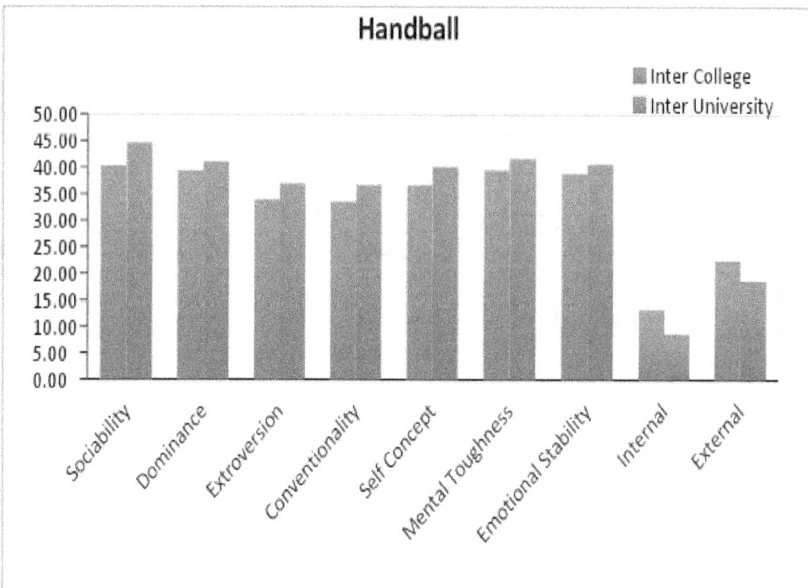

Table 4.8 shows the mean score differences on all these seven personality characteristics as well as Internal and External locus of control between the female sport-persons of Judo participating at Inter-College and Inter-University level competition.

Table 4.8 Mean, SD and t-ratios of personality characteristics of female Judo players of inter college and inter university level competition

Variables	Institute	N	Mean	SDs	SE_B	t-value	df	p-value
Sociability	College	50	44.52	5.44	0.77	1.179	98	0.241
	University	50	43.32	4.71	0.67			
Dominance	College	50	43.12	2.94	0.42	2.055*	98	0.043*
	University	50	41.64	4.16	0.59			
Extraversion	College	50	37.24	4.63	0.65	1.143	98	0.256
	University	50	36.20	4.47	0.63			
Conventionality	College	50	36.50	3.90	0.55	0.053	98	0.958
	University	50	36.46	3.63	0.51			
Self Concept	College	50	39.92	5.33	0.75	0.531	98	0.597
	University	50	39.36	5.22	0.74			
Mental Toughness	College	50	40.80	3.82	0.54	0.942	98	0.349
	University	50	40.08	3.83	0.54			
Emotional Stability	College	50	43.28	4.71	0.67	1.589	98	0.115
	University	50	41.80	4.60	0.65			
Internal LOC	College	50	11.14	6.06	0.86	1.560	98	0.122
	University	50	9.50	4.31	0.61			
External LOC	College	50	22.30	6.91	0.98	0.890	98	0.376
	University	50	23.44	5.86	0.83			

*Significant at 0.05 level (t should be between 1.96 and 2.58)

As per the above table, significant differences could not be noticed on almost all the personality traits between college and university level female sport-persons of Judo game, except the Dominance trait ($t=2.055$, $p< 0.043$) ,where college level players were found to be better on this trait of personality with mean of 43.12 as compared to their university counterparts having mean of 41.64. On all other variables, college and university level female players were having the same level of personality characteristics.

The mean scores of all personality characteristics of Inter-College and Inter-University level female sports-persons of Judo game have been depicted graphically through histogram shown in the Figure 4.5

Figure 4.5 Histogram showing the mean scores of all personality characteristics of Inter-College and Inter-University female sports-persons of Judo game

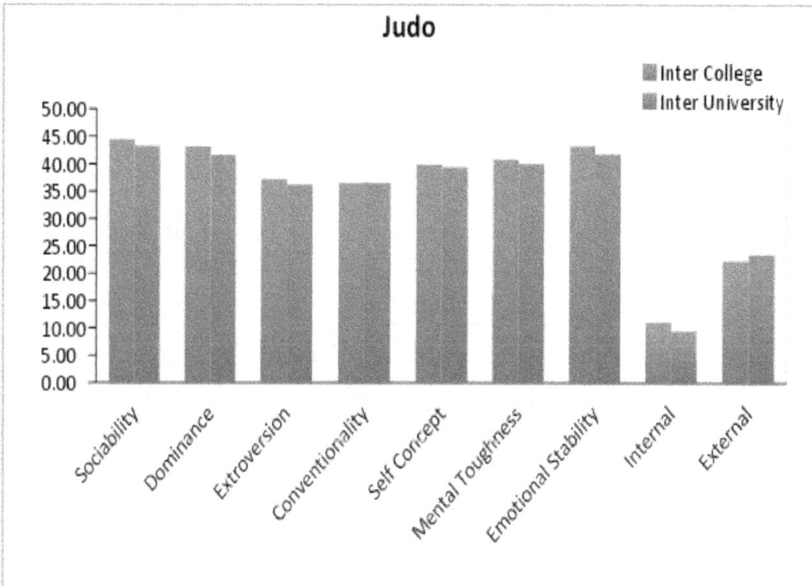

Table 4.9 shows the mean score differences on all these seven personality characteristics as well as Internal and External locus of control between the female sport-persons of Taekwondo game participating at Inter-College and Inter-University level competition.

Table 4.9 Mean, SD and t-ratios of personality characteristics of Taekwondo female players of inter college and inter university level competition

Variables	Institute	N	Mean	SDs	SE_B	t-value	df	p-value
Sociability	College	50	44.74	5.59	0.79	3.81**	98	0.000**
	University	50	40.64	5.16	0.73			
Dominance	College	50	41.48	3.39	0.48	2.60**	98	0.011*
	University	50	39.52	4.09	0.58			
Extraversion	College	50	37.32	5.46	0.77	2.99**	98	0.003**
	University	50	34.28	4.66	0.66			
Conventionality	College	50	35.60	4.34	0.61	1.950	98	0.054
	University	50	34.04	3.63	0.51			
Self Concept	College	50	39.06	4.32	0.61	1.823	98	0.071
	University	50	37.46	4.46	0.63			
Mental Toughness	College	50	42.24	4.76	0.67	4.33**	98	0.000**
	University	50	38.50	3.81	0.54			
Emotional Stability	College	50	42.20	5.19	0.73	3.62**	98	0.000**
	University	50	38.72	4.36	0.62			
Internal LOC	College	50	7.38	3.74	0.53	6.61**	98	0.000**
	University	50	12.06	3.33	0.47			
External LOC	College	50	22.00	6.35	0.90	0.697	98	0.487
	University	50	22.72	3.61	0.51			

** Significant at 0.01 level (t should be more than 2.58)

As per the above table, significant differences between female sportspersons on Inter-College and Inter-University level participation in Taekwondo game were observed on Sociability ($t= 3.813$, $p< 0.001$), Dominance ($t= 2.609$, $p<0.011$), Extraversion ($t=2.993$, $p <0.003$), Mental Toughness ($t= 4.337$, $p<0.001$), Emotional Stability ($t=3.628$, $p<0.001$) and External LOC ($t=6.614$, $p< 0.487$) except in case of

Conventionality, self concept and External LOC, where t values were not statistically significant. The mean scores indicate that college level players got higher mean scores on Sociability (M=44.74), Dominance (M=41.48), Extraversion (M=37.32), Mental Toughness (M=42.24) and Emotional Stability (M=42.20) as compared to their university level counterparts whose mean scores were 40.64, 39.52, 34.28, 38.50 & 38.72 respectively. But in the case of Internal locus of control, university level players were found to be better (M=12.06) than their college counterparts (M= 7.38).

The mean scores of all personality characteristics of Inter-College and Inter-University level female sports-persons of Taekwondo game have been depicted graphically through histogram given in the Figure 4.6

Figure 4.6 Histogram showing the mean scores of all personality characteristics of Inter-College and Inter-University female sports-persons of Taekwondo game

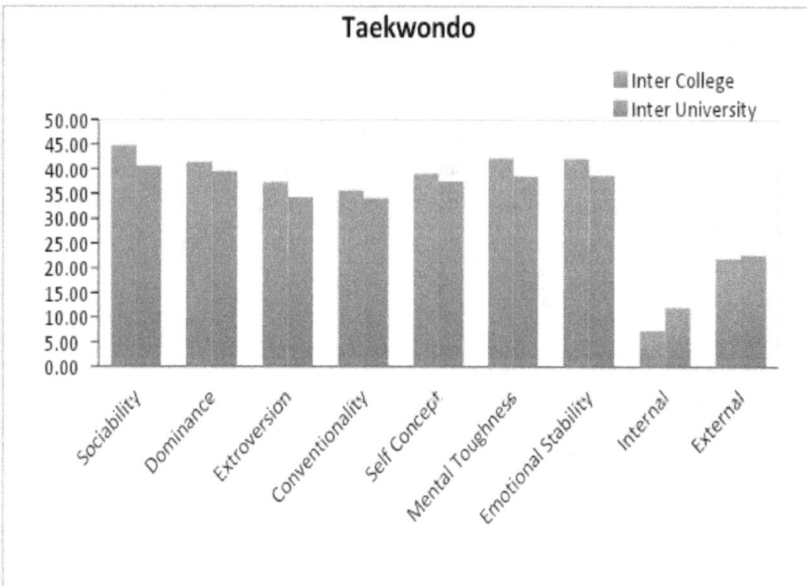

Table 4.10 shows the mean scores differences on all these seven personality characteristics as well as Internal and External locus of control between the female sport-persons of Wrestling game participating at Inter-College and Inter-University level competition.

Table 4.10 Mean, SD and t-ratios of personality characteristics of female Wrestlers of inter college and inter university level competition

Variables	Institute	N	Mean	SDs	SE	t-value	df	p-value
Sociability	College	50	44.86	7.98	1.13	2.76**	98	0.007**
	University	50	41.26	4.62	0.65			
Dominance	College	50	40.82	4.56	0.65	0.361	98	0.719
	University	50	40.52	3.70	0.52			
Extraversion	College	50	36.32	5.24	0.74	1.351	98	0.180
	University	50	35.12	3.46	0.49			
Conventionality	College	50	36.24	5.39	0.76	1.135	98	0.259
	University	50	35.18	3.81	0.54			
Self Concept	College	50	40.28	5.18	0.73	1.875	98	0.064
	University	50	38.50	4.27	0.60			
Mental Toughness	College	50	40.36	4.62	0.65	1.400	98	0.165
	University	50	39.24	3.26	0.46			
Emotional Stability	College	50	40.70	5.20	0.73	0.108	98	0.914
	University	50	40.60	4.02	0.57			
Internal LOC	College	50	7.28	3.40	0.48	2.485*	98	0.015*
	University	50	9.10	3.90	0.55			
External LOC	College	50	25.10	5.30	0.75	0.742	98	0.460
	University	50	25.88	5.22	0.74			

*Significant at 0.05 level (t should be between 1.96 and 2.58)
**Significant at 0.01 level (t should be more than 2.58)

As per the above table, significant differences were found on Sociability (t=2.781, p< 0.007) and Internal LOC (t=2.485, p< 0.015)between the female players of college and university level of Wrestling game, but not on any other personality characteristics, as their t-values were not statistically significant. The mean scores indicate that college level players were getting higher mean scores (B =44.86) on Sociability than university level players (M=41.26). But on Internal LOC, university players got mean score of 9.10 as compared to college players having mean of 7.28.On all other traits of personality, college and university level players were having almost the same level of mean scores.

The mean scores of all personality characteristics of Inter-College and Inter-University level female sports-persons of Wrestling have been depicted graphically through histogram given in the Figure 4.7

Figure 4.7 Histogram showing the mean scores of all personality characteristics of Inter-College and Inter-University female sports-persons of Wrestling

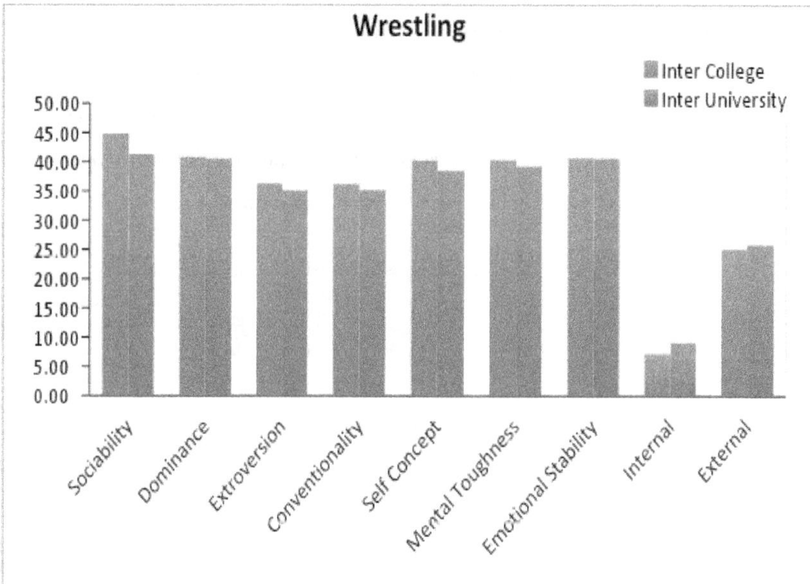

4.3 COMPARISON BETWEEN BALL GAMES AND COMBAT SPORTS ON PERSONALITY CHARACTERISTICS

Another objective of the present study was to make comparison of seven traits of personality as well as Internal and External locus of control between female sportspersons of ball games and Combat Sports. The ball games consisted of Baseball, Football and Handball. All these three are team games. On the other hand, Combat Sports were Judo, Taekwondo and Wrestling which are individual games. It means that comparison were made between team games and individual games female players of Inter-College and Inter-University level competition female sports-persons on seven traits of personality, i.e. Sociability, Dominance, Extraversion, Self-Concept, Conventionality, Mental Toughness and Emotional Stability as well as Internal and External locus of control. In order to achieve this objective, mean scores and standard deviation scores were calculated for all the variables under study for the female players of ball games and Combat Sports separately and then t-ratios were computed in order to find out if significant differences existed and if so at what level of significance.

Table 4.11 shows the mean, SD and t-ratios of scores of different personality characteristics between female sportspersons of ball games and Combat Sports.

Table 4.11 Mean, SD and t-ratios of personality characteristics of female Sportspersons of Ball Games and Combat Sports

Variables	Sports	N	Mean	SDs	SE	t-value	df	p-value
Sociability	Ball Game	300	42.92	5.817	0.335	0.634	598	0.526
	Combat sports	300	43.22	5.897	0.340			
Dominance	Ball Game	300	40.41	4.455	0.257	2.225*	598	0.026*
	Combat sports	300	41.18	3.970	0.229			
Extraversion	Ball Game	300	35.68	5.254	0.303	0.975	598	0.330
	Combat sports	300	36.08	4.785	0.276			
Conventional	Ball Game	300	35.41	4.381	0.252	0.731	598	0.465
	Combat sports	300	35.67	4.219	0.243			
Self Concept	Ball Game	300	3.75	5.328	0.307	0.832	598	0.406
	Combat sports	300	39.09	4.867	0.281			
Mental Toughness	Ball Game	300	40.21	4.981	0.287	0.018	598	0.986
	Combat sports	300	40.20	4.186	0.241			
Emotional Stability	Ball Game	300	40.29	5.444	0.314	2.196*	598	0.028*
	Combat sports	300	41.21	4.877	0.281			
Internal	Ball Game	300	9.93	4.927	0.284	1.343	598	0.180
	Combat sports	300	9.41	4.549	0.262			
External	Ball Game	300	23.46	7.131	0.411	0.201	598	0.841
	Combat sports	300	23.57	5.773	0.333			

*Significant at 0.05 level (t should be between 1.96 and 2.58)

As per the table 4.11, significant differences were not observed on many variables between ball games and Combat Sports players except Dominance and Emotional Stability traits of personality, as t-values of 2.225 and 2.196 were found to be significant at 0.05 level of confidence. On these traits, Combat Sports players were found better (M= 41.183 & 41.216) than ball games players (M=40.416 & 40.290). On all others traits, ball games and Combat Sports players were at the same level, as significant differences were not found statistically.

The mean scores of all personality characteristics of female sports-persons of ball games and Combat Sports have been depicted graphically through histogram given in the Figure 4.8

Figure 4.8: Histogram showing the mean scores of all personality characteristics of female sports-persons in Ball games and Combat Sports

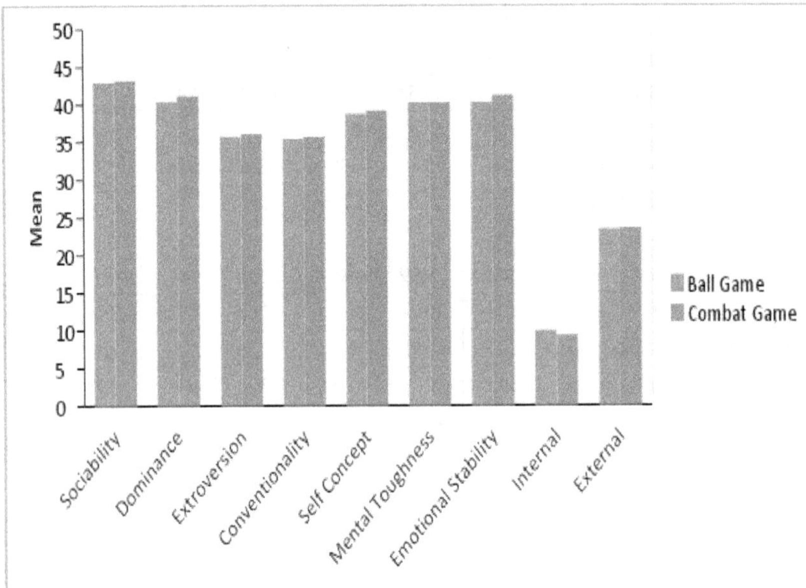

An attempt was also made here to find out the significant differences on the personality characteristics between ball games and team games female players participating at Inter-College and Inter-University level competition separately.

Table 4.12 shows the mean, SD and t-ratios of scores of different personality characteristics between female sportspersons of ball games and Combat Sports at Inter-College level competition.

Table 4.12 Mean, SD and t-ratios of personality characteristics of female Sportspersons of Ball Games and Combat Sports participating at Inter-College level competition

Variables	Sports	N	Mean	SDs	SE	t-value	df	p-value
Sociability	Ball Game	150	41.86	5.957	0.486	3.98**	298	0.000**
	Combat sports	150	44.70	6.401	0.522			
Dominance	Ball Game	150	39.91	4.706	0.384	3.83**	298	0.000**
	Combat sports	150	41.80	3.796	0.309			
Extraversion	Ball Game	150	35.11	5.466	0.446	3.02**	298	0.003**
	Combat sports	150	36.96	5.109	0.417			
Conventionality	Ball Game	150	34.62	4.321	0.352	2.89**	298	0.004**
	Combat sports	150	36.11	4.572	0.373			
Self Concept	Ball Game	150	37.76	5.586	0.456	3.26**	298	0.001**
	Combat sports	150	39.75	4.956	0.404			
Mental Toughness	Ball Game	150	40.02	5.459	0.445	1.934	298	0.054
	Combat sports	150	41.13	4.462	0.364			
Emotional Stability	Ball Game	150	39.99	5.589	0.456	3.34**	298	0.001**
	Combat sports	150	42.06	5.116	0.417			
Internal LOC	Ball Game	150	10.24	4.970	0.405	2.88**	298	0.004**
	Combat sports	150	8.60	4.871	0.397			
External LOC	Ball Game	150	25.72	7.453	0.608	3.23**	298	0.001**
	Combat sports	150	23.13	6.336	0.517			

**Significant at 0.01 level (t should be more than 2.58)

As per the above table, significant differences were found between ball games and combat sports female players of Inter-College level competition on almost all the personality characteristics except only one i.e. Mental Toughness, where the difference was not significant statistically (t=1.934 NS) On the other hand, differences were found to be significant for Sociability (t=3.987, p<0.001), Dominance (t=3.835, p<0.001), Extraversion (t=3.023, p<0.003), Conventionality (t=2.894, p<0.004), Self-Concept (t=3.269, p<0.001),Emotionality Stability (t=3.340, p<0.001), Internal LOC (t=2.886, p<0.004), External LOC (t=3.238, p<0.001). The mean scores indicate that the Combat Sports female players of Inter-College were getting higher mean score on the seven personality characteristics e.g. on Sociability (M=44.706). Dominance (M=41.806) Extraversion (M=36.96), Conventionality (M=36.113), Self-Concept (M=39.753), Emotional Stability (M=42.04) than the ball game players whose mean scores can be compared as 41.86 for Sociability, 39.913 for Dominance, 35.113 for Extraversion, 34.626 for Conventionality, 37.76 for Self-Concept, 39.993 for Emotional Stability. But on the Internal and External locus of control variables, ball games players scored higher than combat sports players, as they can be compared as 10.24 & 8.60 in case of Internal LOC and 25.72 & 23.133 for External LOC.

The mean scores of all personality characteristics of female sports-persons of ball games and combat sports at Inter-College level have been depicted graphically through histogram which given in the Figure 4.9

Figure 4.9 Histogram showing the mean scores of all personality characteristics of female sports-persons of Ball games and sports at Inter-College level

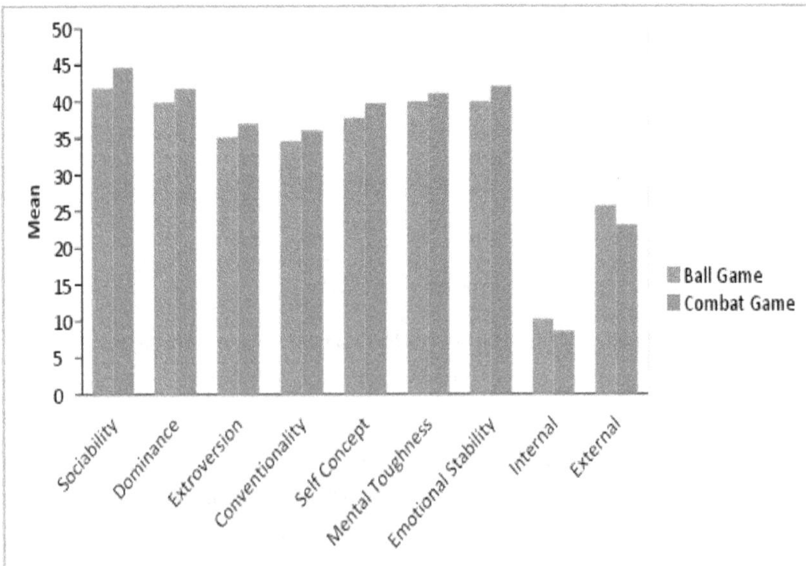

Table 4.13 shows the mean, SD and t-ratios of scores of different personality characteristics between female sportspersons of ball games and combat sports at Inter-University level competition.

Table 4.13 Mean, SD and t-ratios of personality characteristics of female Sportspersons of Ball Games and Combat Sports participating at Inter-University level competition

Sports		N	Mean	SDs	SE	t-value	df	p-value
Sociability	Ball Game	150	43.98	5.491	0.448	3.71**	298	0.000**
	Combat Sports	150	41.74	4.937	0.403			
Dominance	Ball Game	150	40.92	4.144	0.338	0.761	298	0.448
	Combat Sports	150	40.56	4.054	0.331			
Extraversion	Ball Game	150	36.24	4.987	0.407	1.951	298	0.052
	Combat Sports	150	35.20	4.275	0.349			
Conventionality	Ball Game	150	36.20	4.311	0.352	2.075*	298	0.039*
	Combat Sports	150	35.22	3.797	0.310			
Self Concept	Ball Game	150	39.74	4.877	0.398	2.350*	298	0.019*
	Combat Sports	150	38.44	4.702	0.383			
Mental Toughness	Ball Game	150	40.40	4.460	0.364	2.387*	298	0.018*
	Combat Sports	150	39.27	3.676	0.300			
Emotional Stability	Ball Game	150	40.58	5.296	0.432	0.376	298	0.707
	Combat Sports	150	40.37	4.486	0.366			
Internal LOC	Ball Game	150	9.62	4.880	0.398	1.158	298	0.248
	Combat Sports	150	10.22	4.059	0.331			
External LOC	Ball Game	150	21.21	6.024	0.491	4.33**	298	0.000**
	Combat Sports	150	24.01	5.133	0.412			

*Significant at 0.05 level (t should be between 1.96 and 2.58)
**Significant at 0.01 level (t should be more than 2.58)

As per the above table, significant differences were observed in case of Sociability (t=3.715, p<0.001), Conventionality (t=2.075, p<0.039), Self-Concept (t=2.35, p<0.019), Mental Toughness (t=2,387 p<0.018) and External locus of control (t=4.333, p<0.001), whereas in case of Dominance, Extraversion, Emotional Stability and

Internal LOC, no differences were significant statistically. The mean scores indicate that on the personality traits like Sociability, Conventionality, Self-Concept and Mental Toughness, ball games players were getting higher mean scores as 43.98, 36.20, 39.74, 40.40 than the combat sports players whose mean scores were as 41.74, 35.22, 38.44, 39.27 respectively. But on the other hand, combat sports players got more mean scores on External LOC (M=24.013) than the ball game players (M=21.213). On all other variables both ball game and combat game players were having the same level of characteristics.

The mean scores of all personality characteristics of female sports-persons of ball games and Combat Sports at Inter-University level have been depicted graphically through histogram given in the Figure 4.10

Figure 4.10 Histogram showing the mean scores of all personality characteristics of female sports-persons of Ball games and Combat sports at Inter-University level

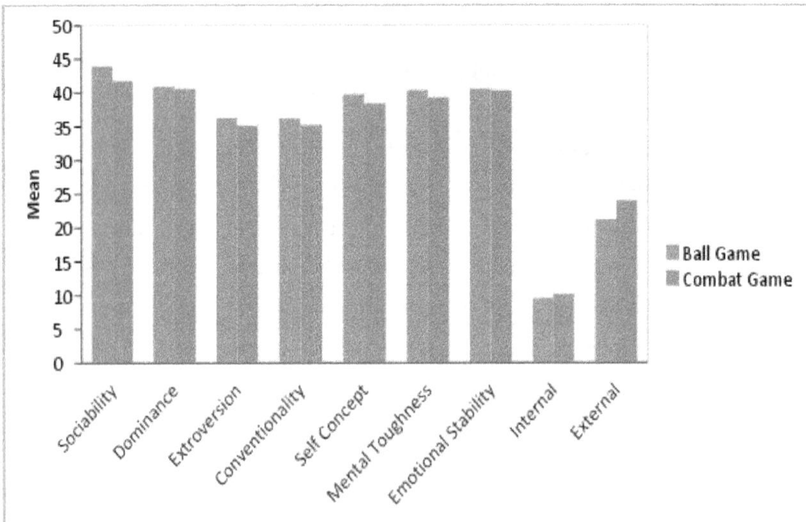

4.4 COMPARISON AMONG FEMALE SPORTSPERSON OF DIFFERENT GAMES ON PERSONALITY CHARACTERISTICS

Another objective of the study was to know the differences on Sociability, Dominance, Extraversion, Self-Concept, Conventionality, Mental Toughness and Emotional Stability as well as Internal and External locus of control among the female sportspersons of different games, e.g. Baseball, Football, Handball, Judo, Taekwondo, and Wrestling. For this purpose, ANOVA technique was applied to find out the F-ratios on the scores of all the personality characteristics one by one, comparing the mean score differences among the female sports-persons of six games participating in the Inter-College and Inter-University level competition. These results have been given in the following tables.

Table 4.14.1 shows the descriptive statistics of the scores of Sociability trait of personality of female sports-persons of Inter-College level competition of six games, i.e. Baseball, Football, Handball, Judo, Taekwondo and Wrestling.

Table 4.14.1 Descriptive Statistics of Sociability Trait of Inter-College female players of six games

Games	N	Mean	Std. Deviation	Std. Error
Baseball	50	42.98	5.223	0.738
Football	50	42.24	6.973	0.986
Handball	50	40.36	5.317	0.752
Judo	50	44.52	5.444	0.769
Taekwondo	50	44.74	5.587	0.7901
Wrestling	50	44.86	7.979	1.128
Total	300	43.28	6.335	0.365

As per the above table, the mean and standard deviation scores of Sociability of the players of six games were as Baseball (42.98±5.22), Football (42.24±6.97), Handball

(40.36±5.31), Judo (44.52±5.44), Taekwondo (44.74±5.58), Wrestling (44.86±7/97) respectively. Table 4.14.2 shows the results of Analysis of Variance of scores of Sociability of female sportspersons who have participated at Inter-College level competition.

Table 4.14.2 Summary Table of ANOVA of Sociability scores of Inter-College female players of six games

Source of Variation	Sum of Sq.	df	Mean Sum of Sq.	F-value	p-value
Between	793.177	5	158.635	4.161**	0.001**
Within	11207.740	294	38.122		
Total	12000.917	299			

** Significant at 0.01 level.

As per the above table, F value of 4.161 was found to be significant at 0.01 level of confidence. It means that there were significant differences in the mean scores of Sociability trait among the players of six games of Inter-College level competition. Now in order to know in which two games significant differences existed, post hoc Analysis of Variance was applied to the mean scores of Sociability of six games players. Baseball players were compared with the players of Football, Handball, Judo, Taekwondo and Wrestling. Similarly the players of other games e.g. Football, Handball, Judo, Taekwondo and Wrestling were compared with the players of all other games by comparing two games one by one.

Table 4.14.3 shows the multiple comparisons of the mean scores of Sociability of female players of six games of Inter-College level competition with each other.

Table 4.14.3. Multiple Comparisons of Mean scores of Sociability Trait of Inter-College Female Players of Six Games

(I) Sports		Mean Difference (I-J)	Std. Error	Sig.	95% Confidence Interval	
					Lower Bound	Upper Bound
Baseball	Football	0.74	1.234	0.549	-1.6903	3.1703
	Handball	2.62^{*}	1.234	0.035*	0.1897	5.0503
	Judo	-1.54	1.234	0.213	-3.9703	0.8903
	Taekwondo	-1.76	1.234	0.155	-4.1903	0.6703
	Wrestling	-1.88	1.234	0.129	-4.3103	0.5503
Football	Handball	1.88	1.234	0.129	-0.5503	4.3103
	Judo	-2.28	1.234	0.066	-4.7103	0.1503
	Taekwondo	-2.50^{*}	1.234	0.044*	-4.9303	-0.0697
	Wrestling	-2.62^{*}	1.234	0.035*	-5.0503	-0.1897
Handball	Judo	-4.16^{**}	1.234	0.001**	-6.5903	-1.7297
	Taekwondo	-4.38^{**}	1.234	0.001**	-6.8103	-1.9497
	Wrestling	-4.50^{**}	1.234	0.001**	-6.9303	-2.0697
Judo	Taekwondo	0-.22	1.234	0.859	-2.6503	2.2103
	Wrestling	0-.34	1.234	0.783	-2.7703	2.0903

* Significant at 0.05 level
** Significant at 0.01 level.

As per the above table, significant differences existed between the Baseball and Handball ($p < 0.035$); Football and Taekwondo ($p<0.044$),Football and Wrestling ($p<0.035$); Handball with Judo ($p<0.001$), Taekwondo ($p<0.001$) and Wrestling ($p<0.001$) and not with players of other games of Inter-College competition. Their mean scores indicate that Baseball players (M=42.98) were better on Sociability than Handball players (M=40.36); Taekwondo players (M=44.74) were better than Football players (M=42.24), Wrestlers (M=44.86) were better than Footballers (M=42.24), Judo (M=44.52), Taekwondo (M= 44.74) as well as Handball players (M=40.36).

Table 4.15.1 shows the descriptive statistics of the scores of Dominance trait of personality of female sports-persons of Inter-College level competition of six games, i.e. Baseball, Football, Handball, Judo, Taekwondo and Wrestling.

Table 4.15.1 Descriptive Statistics of Dominance Trait of Inter-College female players of six games

Games	N	Mean	Std. Dev.	Std. Error
Baseball	50	40.90	5.088	0.719
Football	50	39.38	5.321	0.752
Handball	50	39.46	3.411	0.482
Judo	50	43.12	2.939	0.415
Taekwondo	50	41.48	3.394	0.480
Wrestling	50	40.82	4.561	0.645
Total	300	40.86	4.372	0.252

As per the above table, the mean and standard deviation scores of Dominance of the players of six games as Baseball (40.90 ± 5.08), Football (39.38±5.32), Handball (39.46±3.41), Judo (43.12±2.93), Taekwondo (41.48±3.39) and Wrestling (40.82±4.56).

Table 4.15.2 shows the results of Analysis of Variance of scores of Dominance of female sportspersons who have participated at Inter-College level competition.

Table 4.15.2 Summary Table of ANOVA of Dominance scores of Inter-College female players of six games

Source of Variation	**Sum of Sq.**	**df**	**Mean Sum of Sq.**	**F-value**	**p-value**
Between	482.280	5	96.456	5.418**	0.0001**
Within	5233.840	294	17.802		
Total	5716.120	299			

** Significant at 0.01 level

As per the table 4.15.2, F value of 5.418 was found to be significant at 0.01 level of confidence. It means that there were significant differences in the mean scores of Dominance among the female players of six games of Inter-College level competition. Now in order to know in which two games significant differences existed, post hoc Analysis of Variance was applied to the mean scores of Dominance of six games players. Baseball players were compared with the players of Football, Handball, Judo, Taekwondo and Wrestling. Similarly the players of other games e.g. Football, Handball, Judo, Taekwondo and Wrestling were compared with the players of all other games by comparing two games one by one. Table 4.15.3 shows the multiple comparisons of the mean scores of Dominance trait of female players of six games of Inter-College level competition with each other.

Table 4.15.3. Multiple Comparisons of Mean scores of Dominance Trait of Inter-College Female Players of Six Games

(I) Sports		Mean Difference (I-J)	Std. Error	Sig.	95% Confidence Interval	
					Lower Bound	Upper Bound
Baseball	Football	1.52	0.843	0.073	-0.1408	3.1808
	Handball	1.44	0.843	0.089	-0.2208	3.1008
	Judo	-2.22*	0.843	0.009**	-3.8808	-0.5592
	Taekwondo	-0.58	0.843	0.492	-2.2408	1.0808
	Wrestling	0.08	0.843	0.925	-1.5808	1.7408
Football	Handball	0-.08	0.843	0.925	-1.7408	1.5808
	Judo	-3.74*	0.843	0.0001**	-5.4008	-2.0792
	Taekwondo	-2.10*	0.843	0.013*	-3.7608	-0.4392
	Wrestling	-1.44	0.843	0.089	-3.1008	0.2208
Handball	Judo	-3.66*	0.843	0.0001**	-5.3208	-1.9992
	Taekwondo	-2.02*	0.843	0.017*	-3.6808	-0.3592
	Wrestling	-1.36	0.843	0.108	-3.0208	0.3008
Judo	Taekwondo	1.64	0.843	0.053	-0.0208	3.3008
	Wrestling	2.30*	0.843	0.007**	0.6392	3.9608
Taekwondo	Wrestling	0.66	0.843	0.435	-1.0008	2.3208

* The mean difference is significant at the 0.05 level.
** The mean difference is significant at 0.01 level.

As per the table 4.15.3, significant differences existed between the Baseball and Judo ($p< 0.009$), Football and Judo ($p<0.001$), Football and Taekwondo ($p<0.013$), Handball with Judo ($p<0.001$), Handball and Taekwondo ($p<0.017$)as well as Judo and

Wrestling ($p<0.007$) and not with the players of other games of Inter-College competition. Their mean scores indicate that the Judo players (M=43.12) were better than Baseball players (M=40.90), and Football players (M=39.38) and Handball players (M=39.46) and Wrestling (M=40.82) and Taekwondo players (M=41.48) but Taekwondo players were better than Football players (M=39.38).

Table 4.16.1 shows the descriptive statistics of the scores of Extraversion trait of personality of female sports-persons of Inter-College level competition of six games, i.e. Baseball, Football, Handball, Judo, Taekwondo and Wrestling.

Table 4.16.1 Descriptive Statistics of Extraversion Trait of Inter-College female players of six games

Games	N	Mean	Std. Dev.	Std. Error
Baseball	50	36.26	5.201	0.735
Football	50	35.12	6.215	0.879
Handball	50	33.96	4.742	0.670
Judo	50	37.24	4.627	0.654
Taekwondo	50	37.32	5.463	0.772
Wrestling	50	36.32	5.242	0.741
Total	300	36.03	5.362	0.309

As per the above table, the means and standard deviation scores of Extraversion of the female players of six games as Baseball (36.26±5.20), Football (35.12 ±6.21), Handball (33.96±4.74), Judo (37.24±4.62), Taekwondo (37.32±5.46), Wrestling (36.32±5.24) respectively.

Table 4.16.2 shows the results of Analysis of Variance of scores of Extraversion trait of female sportspersons who have participated at Inter-College level competition.

Table 4.16.2 Summary Table of ANOVA of Extraversion scores of Inter-College female players of six games

Source of Variation	**Sum of Sq.**	**df**	**Mean Sum of Sq.**	**F-value**	**p-value**
Between	418.897	5	83.779	3.011**	0.011**
Within	8179.700	294	27.822		
Total	8598.597	299			

** Significant at 0.01 level

As per the above table, F value of 3.011 was found to be significant at 0.01 level of confidence. It means that there were significant differences in the mean scores of Extraversion among the female players of six games of Inter-College level competition. Now in order to know in which two games significant differences existed, post hoc Analysis of Variance was applied to the mean scores of Extraversion trait of six games players. Baseball players were compared with the players of Football, Handball, Judo, Taekwondo and Wrestling. Similarly the players of other games e.g. Football, Handball, Judo, Taekwondo and Wrestling were compared with the players of all other games by comparing two games one by one.

Table 4.16.3 shows the multiple comparisons of the mean scores of Extraversion Trait of female players of six games of Inter-College level competition with each other.

Table 4.16.3. Multiple Comparisons of Mean scores of Extraversion Trait of Inter-College Female Players of Six Games

(I) Games		Mean Difference (I-J)	Std. Error	Sig.	95% Confidence Interval	
					Lower Bound	Upper Bound
Baseball	Football	1.14	1.054	0.281	-0.9362	3.2162
	Handball	2.30*	1.054	0.030*	0.2238	4.3762
	Judo	-0.98	1.054	0.354	-3.0562	1.0962
	Taekwondo	-1.06	1.054	0.316	-3.1362	1.0162
	Wrestling	0-.06	1.054	0.955	-2.1362	2.0162
Football	Handball	1.16	1.054	0.272	-0.9162	3.2362
	Judo	-2.12*	1.054	0.045*	-4.1962	-0.0438
	Taekwondo	-2.20*	1.054	0.038*	-4.2762	-0.1238
	Wrestling	-1.20	1.054	0.256	-3.2762	0.8762
Handball	Judo	-3.28**	1.054	0.002**	-5.3562	-1.2038
	Taekwondo	-3.36**	1.054	0.002**	-5.4362	-1.2838
	Wrestling	-2.36*	1.054	0.026*	-4.4362	-0.2838
Judo	Taekwondo	0-.08	1.054	0.940	-2.1562	1.9962
	Wrestling	0.92	1.054	0.384	-1.1562	2.9962
Taekwondo	Wrestling	1.00	1.054	0.344	-1.0762	3.0762

* The mean difference is significant at the 0.05 level.
** The mean difference is significant at the 0.01 level.

As per the above table, significant differences existed between the players of Baseball and Handball ($p < 0.030$); Football and Judo ($p<0.045$), Football and Taekwondo ($p<0.038$); Handball with Judo ($p<0.002$), Taekwondo ($p<0.002$) and Wrestling (p<0.026); and not with the players of other games of Inter-College competition. Their mean scores indicate that the Baseball players (M=36.26) were better than Handball players (M=33.96), and Judo players (M=37.24) were better than Football players (M=35.12) and Handball players (M=33.96). Taekwondo players (M=37.32) were better than Footballers (M=35.12), Judo players (M=37.24) were better than, Taekwondo players (M=37.32) as well as wrestlers (M=36.32) were better than Handball players (M=33.96).

Table 4.17.1 shows the descriptive statistics of the scores of Conventionality trait of personality of female sports-persons of Inter-College level competition of six games, i.e. Baseball, Football, Handball, Judo, Taekwondo and Wrestling.

Table 4.17.1 Descriptive Statistics of Conventionality Trait of Inter-College female players of six games

Games	N	Mean	Std. Dev.	Std. Error
Baseball	50	36.02	4.027	0.569
Football	50	34.24	4.684	0.662
Handball	50	33.62	3.932	0.556
Judo	50	36.50	3.897	0.551
Taekwondo	50	35.60	4.342	0.614
Wrestling	50	36.24	5.392	0.762
Total	300	35.37	4.503	0.260

As per the above table, the mean and standard deviation scores of Conventionality trait of personality of the female players of six games were as Baseball (36.02 ± 4.02), Football (34.24 ± 4.68), Handball (33.62 ± 3.93), Judo (36.50 ± 3.89), Taekwondo (35.60 ± 4.34), Wrestling (36.24 ± 5.39) respectively.

Table 4.17.2 shows the results of Analysis of Variance of scores of Conventionality of female sports-persons who had participated at Inter-College level competition.

Table 4.17.2 Summary Table of ANOVA of Conventionality scores of Inter-College female players of six games

Source of Variation	Sum of Sq.	df	Mean Sum of Sq.	F-value	p-value
Between	342.430	5	68.486	3.519**	0.004**
Within	5721.500	294	19.461		
Total	6063.930	299			

** Significant at 0.01 level.

As per the above table, F value of 3.519 was found to be significant at 0.01 level of confidence. It means that there were significant differences in the mean scores on Conventionality Trait among the female players of six games of Inter-College level competition. Now in order to know in which two games significant differences existed, post hoc Analysis of Variance was applied to the mean scores of Conventionality trait of six games players. Baseball players were compared with the players of Football, Handball, Judo, Taekwondo and Wrestling. Similarly the players of other games e.g. Football, Handball, Judo, Taekwondo and Wrestling were compared with the players of all other games by comparing two games one by one.

Table 4.17.3 shows the multiple comparisons of the mean scores of Conventionality trait of female players of six games of Inter-College level competition with each other.

Table 4.17.3. Multiple Comparisons of Mean scores of Conventionality of Inter-College Female Players of Six Games

(I) Sports		Mean Difference (I-J)	Std. Error	Sig.	95% Confidence Interval	
					Lower Bound	Upper Bound
Baseball	Football	1.78*	0.882	0.045*	0.0436	3.5164
	Handball	2.40**	0.882	0.007**	0.6636	4.1364
	Judo	-0.48	0.882	0.587	-2.2164	1.2564
	Taekwondo	0.42	0.882	0.634	-1.3164	2.1564
	Wrestling	0-.22	0.882	0.803	-1.9564	1.5164
Football	Handball	0.62	0.882	0.483	-1.1164	2.3564
	Judo	-2.26*	0.882	0.011*	-3.9964	-0.5236
	Taekwondo	-1.36	0.882	0.124	-3.0964	0.3764
	Wrestling	-2.00*	0.882	0.024*	-3.7364	-0.2636
Handball	Judo	-2.88**	0.882	0.001**	-4.6164	-1.1436
	Taekwondo	-1.98*	0.882	0.026*	-3.7164	-0.2436
	Wrestling	-2.62**	0.882	0.003**	-4.3564	-0.8836
Judo	Taekwondo	0.90	0.882	0.309	-0.8364	2.6364
	Wrestling	0.26	0.882	0.768	-1.4764	1.9964
Taekwondo	Wrestling	-0.64	0.882	0.469	-2.3764	1.0964

* The mean difference is significant at the 0.05 level.
** The mean difference is significant at the 0.01 level.

As per the above table, significant differences existed between the Baseball and Football ($p<0.045$), and Handball ($p<0.007$); Football and Judo ($p<0.011$), and Wrestling (p<0.024); Handball with Judo (p<0.001), Taekwondo (p<0.026) and Wrestling (p<0.003) and not with the players of other games of Inter-College competition. Their mean scores indicate that the Baseball players (M=36.02) were better than Football (M=34.24) and Handball players (M=33.62) while Judo players (M=36.50) and Wrestling players (M=36.24) were better than Football players (M=34.24). Judo players (M=36.50) Taekwondo (M=35.60), and Wrestling players (M=36.24) were better than Handball player (M=33.62).

Table 4.18.1 shows the descriptive statistics of the scores of Self-Concept trait of personality of female sports-persons of Inter-College level competition of six games, i.e. Baseball, Football, Handball, Judo, Taekwondo and Wrestling.

Table 4.18.1 Descriptive Statistics of Self-Concept of Inter-College Trait female players of six games

Games	N	Mean	Std, Dev	Std, Dev
Baseball	50	39.32	4.829	0.682
Football	50	37.24	6.364	0.900
Handball	50	36.72	5.213	0.737
Judo	50	39.92	5.329	0.753
Taekwondo	50	39.06	4.316	0.610
Wrestling	50	40.28	5.182	0.732
Total	300	38.75	5.365	0.309

As per the above table, the means and standard deviation scores of Self-Concept trait of personality of the female players of six games were as Baseball (39.32 ± 4.82), Football (37.24 ± 6.36), Handball (36.72 ± 5.21), Judo (39.92 ± 5.32), Taekwondo (39.06 ± 4.31), Wrestling (40.28 ± 5.18) respectively.

Table 4.18.2 shows the results of Analysis of Variance of scores of Self-Concept of female sports-persons who have participated at Inter-College level competition.

Table 4.18.2 Summary Table of ANOVA of Self-Concept scores of Inter-College female players of six games

Source of Variation	Sum of Sq.	df	Mean Sum of Sq.	F-value	p-value
Between	526.577	5	105.315	3.832**	0.002**
Within	8080.660	294	27.485		
Total	8607.237	299			

** Significant at 0. 01 level

As per the above table, F value of 3.832 was found to be significant at 0.01 level of confidence. It means that there were significant differences in the mean scores of Self-Concept among the female players of six games of Inter-College level competition. Now in order to know in which two games significant differences existed, post-hoc Analysis of Variance was applied to the mean scores of Self-Concept of six games players. Baseball players were compared with the players of Football, Handball Judo, Taekwondo and Wrestling. Similarly the players of other games e.g. Football, Handball, Judo, Taekwondo and Wrestling were compared with the players of all other games by comparing two games one by one.

Table 4.18.3 shows the multiple comparisons of the mean scores of Self-Concept of female players of six games of Inter-College level competition with each other.

Table 4.18.3 Multiple Comparisons of Mean scores of Self-Concept of Inter-College Female Players of Six Games

(I) Games		Mean Difference (I-J)	Std. Error	Sig.	95%Confidence Interval	
					Lower Bound	Upper Bound
Baseball	Football	2.080*	1.048	0.048*	0.0164	4.1436
	Handball	2.600*	1.048	0.014*	0.5364	4.6636
	Judo	-0.600	1.048	0.568	-2.6636	1.4636
	Taekwondo	0.260	1.048	0.804	-1.8036	2.3236
	Wrestling	-0.960	1.048	0.361	-3.0236	1.1036
Football	Handball	0.520	1.048	0.620	-1.5436	2.5836
	Judo	-2.680*	1.048	0.011*	-4.7436	-0.6164
	Taekwondo	-1.820	1.048	0.084	-3.8836	0.2436
	Wrestling	-3.040**	1.048	0.004**	-5.1036	-0.9764
Handball	Judo	-3.200**	1.048	0.002**	-5.2636	-1.1364
	Taekwondo	-2.340*	1.048	0.026*	-4.4036	-0.2764
	Wrestling	-3.560**	1.048	0.001**	-5.6236	-1.4964
Judo	Taekwondo	0.860	1.048	0.413	-1.2036	2.9236
	Wrestling	-0.360	1.048	0.732	-2.4236	1.7036
Taekwondo	Wrestling	-1.220	1.048	0.246	-3.2836	0.8436

* The mean difference is significant at the 0.05 level
** The mean. difference is significant at the 0.01 level.

As per the above table, significant differences existed between the Baseball and Football ($p<0.048$), and Handball ($p<0.014$); Football and Judo ($p<0.011$), and Wrestling ($p<0.004$); Handball with Judo ($p<0.002$), Taekwondo ($p<0.026$) and Wrestling (p<0.001) and not with the players of other games of Inter-College competition. Their mean scores indicate that the Baseball players (M=39.32) were better than Football (M=37.24) and Handball players (M=36.72); Judo players (M=39.92) were better than Football players (M=37.24), Handball players (M=36.72) and Taekwondo players (M=39.06). Wrestlers (M=40.28) were better than Footballers and Handball players (M=36.72).

Table 4.19.1 shows the descriptive statistics of the scores of Mental Toughness trait of personality of female sports-persons of Inter-College level competition of six games, i.e. Baseball, Football, Handball, Judo, Taekwondo and Wrestling.

Table 4.19.1 Descriptive Statistics of Mental Toughness Trait of Inter-college female players of six games

Games	N	Mean	St. Dev.	St. Error
Baseball	50	40.66	5.15320	0.72877
Football	50	39.84	6.40268	0.90548
Handball	50	39.56	4.73442	0.66955
Judo	50	40.80	3.81725	0.53984
Taekwondo	50	42.24	4.75764	0.67283
Wrestling	50	40.36	4.62363	0.65388
Total	300	40.57	5.00877	0.28918

As per the above table, the mean and standard deviation scores of Mental Toughness trait of personality of the female players of six games as Baseball (40.66 ± 5.15), Football (39.84 ± 6.40), Handball (39.56 ± 4.73), Judo (40.80 ± 3.81), Taekwondo (42.24 ± 4.75), and Wrestling (40.36 ± 4.62) respectively.

Table 4.19.2 shows the results of Analysis of Variance of scores of Mental Toughness of female sports-persons who have participated at Inter-College level competition.

Table 4.19.2 Summary Table of ANOVA of Mental Toughness scores of Inter-College female players of six games

Source of Variation	Sum of Sq.	df	Mean Sum of Sq.	F-value	p-value
Between	222.337	5	44.467	1.796	0.113
Within	7278.900	294	24.758		
Total	7501.237	299			

As per the above table, F value of 1.796 was not found out to be significant at any level of confidence. It means that there were not any significant differences in the mean scores of Mental Toughness of female sports-persons of Inter-College level competition among the six games, i.e. Baseball, Football, Handball, Judo, Taekwondo and Wrestling. So there was no need of calculating the post-hoc Analysis of Variance on the mean scores of Mental Toughness of players of six games.

Table 4.20.1 shows the descriptive statistics of the scores of Emotional Stability trait of personality of female sports-persons of Inter-College level competition of six games, i.e. Baseball, Football, Handball, Judo, Taekwondo and Wrestling.

Table 4.20.1 Descriptive Statistics of Emotional Stability Trait of Inter-College female players of six games

Games	N	Mean	Std. Dev.	Std. Error
Baseball	50	41.72	5.063	0.716
Football	50	39.32	5.960	0.842
Handball	50	38.94	5.403	0.764
Judo	50	43.28	4.712	0.666
Taekwondo	50	42.20	5.194	0.734
Wrestling	50	40.70	5.195	0.734
Total	300	41.02	5.448	0.314

As per the above table, the mean and standard deviation scores of Emotional Stability trait of personality of the female players of six games were as Baseball (41.72 ± 5.06), Football (39.32 ± 5.96), Handball (38.94 ± 5.40), Judo (43.28 ± 4.71), Taekwondo (42.20 ± 5.19),and Wrestling (40.70 ± 5.19) respectively.

Table 4.20.2 shows the results of Analysis of Variance of scores of Emotional Stability of female sports-persons who have participated at Inter-College level competition.

Table 4.20.2 Summary Table of ANOVA of Emotional Stability scores of Inter-College female players of six games.

Source of Variation	Sum of Sq.	df	Mean Sum of Sq.	F-value	p-value
Between	715.427	5	143.085	5.155**	0.0001**
Within	8160.360	294	27.756		
Total	8875.787	299			

As per the above table, F value of 5.155 was found to be significant at 0.01 level of confidence. It means that there were significant differences in the mean scores of Emotional Stability among the female players of six games of Inter-College level competition. Now in order to know in which two games significant differences existed, post-hoc Analysis of Variance was applied to the mean scores of emotional maturity of six games players. Baseball players were compared with the players of Football, Handball Judo, Taekwondo and Wrestling. Similarly the players of other games e.g.; Football Handball, Judo Taekwondo and Wrestling were compared with the players of all other games by comparing two games one by one.

Table 4.20.3 shows the multiple comparisons of the mean scores of Emotional Stability trait of female players of six games of Inter-College level competition with each other.

Table 4.20.3. Multiple Comparisons of Mean scores of Emotional Stability of Inter-College Female Players of Six Games

(I) Games		Mean Difference (I-J)	Std. Error	Sig.	95% Confidence Interval	
					Lower Bound	Upper Bound
Baseball	Football	2.40*	1.053	0.023*	0.3263	4.4737
	Handball	2.78**	1.053	0.009**	0.7063	4.8537
	Judo	-1.56	1.053	0.140	-3.6337	0.5137
	Taekwondo	-0.48	1.053	0.649	-2.5537	1.5937
	Wrestling	1.02	1.053	0.334	-1.0537	3.0937
Football	Handball	0.38	1.053	0.719	-1.6937	2.4537
	Judo	-3.96**	1.053	0.0001**	-6.0337	-1.8863
	Taekwondo	-2.88**	1.053	0.007**	-4.9537	-0.8063
	Wrestling	-1.38	1.053	0.191	-3.4537	0.6937
Handball	Judo	-4.34**	1.053	0.0001**	-6.4137	-2.2663
	Taekwondo	-3.26**	1.053	0.002**	-5.3337	-1.1863
	Wrestling	-1.76	1.053	0.096	-3.8337	0.3137
Judo	Taekwondo	1.08	1.053	0.306	-0.9937	3.1537
	Wrestling	2.58*	1.053	0.015*	0.5063	4.6537
Taekwondo	Wrestling	1.50	1.053	0.156	-0.5737	3.5737

* The mean difference is significant at the 0.05 level.
** The mean difference is significant at the 0.01 level

As per the above table, significant differences existed between the Baseball with Football ($p< 0.023$), and Handball ($p<0.009$); Football with Judo ($p<0.0001$), and

Taekwondo ($p<0.007$); Handball with Judo ($p<0.0001$), and Taekwondo ($p<0.002$); as well as Judo and Wrestling ($p<0.015$) and not with the players of other games of Inter-College competition. Their mean scores indicate that the Baseball players (M=41.72) were better than Football (M=39.32) and Handball players (M=38.94), and Judo players (M=43.28) were better than Football players (M=39.32) and wrestlers (M=40.70; Taekwondo (M=42.20) were better than Footballers (M=39.32). Judo players (M=43.28) and Taekwondo players (M=42.20) were better than Handball players (M=38.94).

Table 4.21.1 shows the descriptive statistics of the scores of Internal Locus of Control trait of personality of female sports-persons of Inter-College level competition of six games, i.e. Baseball, Football, Handball, Judo, Taekwondo and Wrestling.

Table 4.21.1 Descriptive Statistics of Internal LOC Trait of Inter-College female players of six games

Games	N	Mean	Std. Dev.	Std. Error
Baseball	50	9.02	4.533	0.641
Football	50	8.46	4.380	0.619
Handball	50	13.24	4.631	0.655
Judo	50	11.14	6.060	0.857
Taekwondo	50	7.38	3.735	0.528
Wrestling	50	7.28	3.404	0.481
Total	300	9.42	4.981	0.287

As per the above table, the means and standard deviation scores of Internal LOC trait of personality of the female players of six games were as Baseball (9.02 ± 4.53), Football (8.46 ± 4.38), Handball (13.24 ± 4.63), Judo (11.14 ± 6.06), Taekwondo (7.38 ± 3.73), Wrestling (7.28 ± 3.40) respectively.

Table 4.21.2 shows the results of Analysis of Variance of scores of Internal locus of control of female sports-persons who have participated at Inter-College level competition.

Table 4.21.2

Summary Table of ANOVA of Internal LOC scores of Inter-College female players of six games.

Source of Variation	Sum of Squares	df	Mean Sum of Sq.	F-value	p-value
Between	1368.680	5	273.736	13.301**	0.0001 **
Within	6050.400	294	20.580		
Total	7419.080	299			

** Significant at 0.01 level

As per the above table, F value of 13.30 was found to be significant at 0.01 level of confidence. It means that there were significant differences in the mean scores of Internal locus of control among the female players of six games of Inter-College level competition. Now in order to know in which two games significant differences existed, post-hoc Analysis of Variance was applied to the mean scores of Internal locus of control of six games players. Baseball players were compared with the players of Football, Handball, Judo, Taekwondo and Wrestling. Similarly the players of other games e.g. Football, Handball, Judo Taekwondo and Wrestling were compared with the players of all other games by comparing two games one by one.

Table 4.21.3 shows the multiple comparisons of the mean scores of Internal locus of control trait of female players of six games of Inter-College level competition with each other.

Table 4.21.3.

Multiple Comparisons of Mean scores of Internal LOC of Inter-College Female Players of Six Games

(I) Sports		Mean Difference (I-J)	Std. Error	Sig.	95% Confidence Interval	
					Lower Bound	Upper Bound
Baseball	Football	0.560	0.907	0.538	-1.2256	2.3456
	Handball	-4.220**	0.907	0.0001**	-6.0056	-2.4344
	Judo	-2.120*	0.907	0.020*	-3.9056	-0.3344
	Taekwondo	1.640	0.907	0.072	-0.1456	3.4256
	Wrestling	1.740	0.907	0.056	-0.0456	3.5256
Football	Handball	-4.780**	0.907	0.0001**	-6.5656	-2.9944
	Judo	-2.680**	0.907	0.003**	-4.4656	-0.8944
	Taekwondo	1.080	0.907	0.235	-0.7056	2.8656
	Wrestling	1.180	0.907	0.194	-0.6056	2.9656
Handball	Judo	2.100*	0.907	0.021*	0.3144	3.8856
	Taekwondo	5.860**	0.907	0.0001**	4.0744	7.6456
	Wrestling	5.960**	0.907	0.0001**	4.1744	7.7456
Judo	Taekwondo	3.760**	0.907	0.0001**	1.9744	5.5456
	Wrestling	3.860**	0.907	0.0001**	2.0744	5.6456
Taekwondo	Wrestling	0.100	0.907	0.912	-1.6856	1.8856

* The mean difference is significant at the 0.05 level.

** The mean difference is significant at the 0.01 level.

As per the above table, significant differences existed between the Baseball with Handball ($p<0.001$) and Judo ($p<0.020$); Football with Handball ($p<0.001$) and Judo (p<0.003); and Handball with Judo (p<0.021), Taekwondo (p<0.001) and Wrestling (p<0.001) as well as Judo and Taekwondo (p < 0.001) and Wrestling (p<0.001) and not with the players of other games of Inter-College competition. Their mean scores indicate that the Handball players (M=13.24) and Judo players (M=11.14) were better than Baseball (M=9.02) as well as Football (M=8.46), Taekwondo (M=7.38) and Wrestling (M=7.28) whereas Judo players (M=11.14) were better than Football players (M=8.46) and Taekwondo (M=7.38) and Wrestling (M=7.28).

Table 4.22.1 shows the descriptive statistics of the scores of External Locus of Control trait of personality of female sports-persons of Inter-College level competition of six games, i.e. Baseball, Football, Handball, Judo, Taekwondo and Wrestling.

Table 4.22.1

Descriptive Statistics of External LOC Trait of Inter-College female players of six games

Games	N	Mean	Std. Dev.	Std. Error
Baseball	50	22.14	5.848	0.827
Football	50	32.52	5.894	0.833
Handball	50	22.50	5.399	0.763
Judo	50	22.30	6.911	0.977
Taekwondo	50	22.00	6.350	0.898
Wrestling	50	25.10	5.296	0.749
Total	300	24.42	7.026	0.405

As per the above table, the means and standard deviation scores of External LOC trait of personality of the female players of six games were as Baseball (22.14 ± 5.84), Football (32.52 ± 5.89), Handball (22.50 ± 5.39), Judo (22.30 ± 6.91), Taekwondo (22.00 ± 6.35), and Wrestling (25.10 ± 5.29) respectively.

Table 4.22.2 shows the results of Analysis of Variance of scores of External locus of control of female sports-persons who have participated at Inter-College level competition.

Table 4.22.2 Summary Table of ANOVA of External LOC scores of Inter-College female players of six games.

Source of Variation	Sum of Sq.	df	Mean Sum of Sq.	F-value	p-value
Between	4265.387	5	853.077	23.891**	0.0001**
Within	10498.000	294	35.707		
Total	14763.387	299			

** Significant at 0.01 level of confidence

As per the above table, F value of 23.89 was found to be significant at 0.01 level of confidence. It means that there were significant differences in the mean scores of External locus of control among the female players of six games of Inter-College level competition. Now in order to know in which two games significant differences existed, post-hoc Analysis of Variance was applied to the mean scores of External locus of control of six games players. Baseball players were compared with the players of Football, Handball, Judo, Taekwondo and Wrestling. Similarly the players of other games e.g. Football, Handball, Judo Taekwondo and Wrestling were compared with the players of all other games by comparing two games one by one.

Table 4.22.3 shows the multiple comparisons of the mean scores of External locus of control of female players of six games of Inter-College level competition with each other.

Table 4.22.3 Multiple Comparisons of Mean scores of External LOC of Inter-College Female Players of Six Games

(I) Games		Mean Difference (I-J)	Std. Error	Sig.	95% Confidence Interval	
					Lower Bound	Upper Bound
Baseball	Football	-10.38**	1.195	0.0001**	-12.7321	-8.0279
	Handball	-0.36	1.195	0.763	-2.7121	1.9921
	Judo	-0.16	1.195	0.894	-2.5121	2.1921
	Taekwondo	0.14	1.195	0.907	-2.2121	2.4921
	Wrestling	-2.96*	1.195	0.014*	-5.3121	-0.6079
Football	Handball	10.02**	1.195	0.0001**	7.6679	12.3721
	Judo	10.22**	1.195	0.0001**	7.8679	12.5721
	Taekwondo	10.52**	1.195	0.0001**	8.1679	12.8721
	Wrestling	7.42**	1.195	0.0001**	5.0679	9.7721
Handball	Judo	0.20	1.195	0.867	-2.1521	2.5521
	Taekwondo	0.50	1.195	0.676	-1.8521	2.8521
	Wrestling	-2.60*	1.195	0.030*	-4.9521	-0.2479
Judo	Taekwondo	0.30	1.195	0.802	-2.0521	2.6521
	Wrestling	-2.80*	1.195	0.020*	-5.1521	-0.4479
Taekwondo	Wrestling	-3.10**	1.195	0.010**	-5.4521	-0.7479

* The mean difference is significant at the 0.05 level.
** The mean difference is significant at the 0.01 level

As per the table 4.22.3, significant differences existed between the Baseball with Football ($p<0.001$) and Wrestling ($p<0.014$); Football with Handball ($p<0.001$), Judo ($p<0.001$), Taekwondo ($p<0.001$) and Wrestling ($p<0.001$); Handball with Wrestling ($p<0.030$); Judo with Wrestling ($p<0.020$) and Taekwondo and Wrestling ($p<0.010$), but not with the players of other games of Inter-College competition. Their mean scores indicate that the Football players (M=32.52) and Wrestling (M=25.10) were better than Baseball (M=22.14). Football players (M=32.52) were better than Handball players (M=22.50), Judo (M=22.30), Taekwondo (M=22.00) as well as Wrestling (M=25.10) where as Wrestling players (M=25.10) were better than Handball (M=22.50), Judo (M=22.30) and Taekwondo (M= 22.00).

4.5. COMPARISON AMONG FEMALE SPORTSPERSONS OF DIFFERENT GAMES OF INTER-UNIVERSITY LEVEL COMPETITION

An attempt was made in the present study to compare the female sportspersons of different games who have participated at Inter-University level competition on all the personality characteristics i.e. Sociability, Dominance, Extraversion, Conventionality, Self-Concept, Mental Toughness and Emotionality Stability as well as Internal and External locus of control. As there were six games, three ball games and three Combat Sports, ANOVA technique was applied in order to find out the F-ratios for knowing if significant differences existed and where the significant differences were found and in further to find out the differences between two games, post-hoc Analysis of Variance was applied and then their mean scores were compared to know the female players of which games were better on these psychological characteristics. These results have been given in the following tables.

Table 4.23.1 shows the descriptive statistics of the scores of Sociability trait of personality of female sports-persons of Inter-University level competition of six games, i.e. Baseball, Football, Handball, Judo, Taekwondo and Wrestling.

Table 4.23.1 Descriptive Statistics of Sociability Trait of Inter-University female players of six games

Games	N	Mean	Std. Dev	Std. Error
Baseball	50	42.74	5.865	0.829
Football	50	44.5400	5.803	0.820
Handball	50	44.66	4.609	0.651
Judo	50	43.32	4.709	0.666
Taekwondo	50	40.64	5.157	0.729
Wrestling	50	41.26	4.619	0.653
Total	300	42.86	5.332	0.307

As per the above table, the means and standard deviation scores of Sociability of the players of six games were as Baseball (42.74 ±5.86), Football (44.54 ± 5.80), Handball (44.66±4.60), Judo (43.32±4.70), Taekwondo (40.64 ± 5.15), and Wrestling (41.26 ±4.61) respectively.

Table 4.23.2 shows the results of Analysis of Variance of scores of Sociability of female sportspersons who have participated at Inter-University level competition.

Table 4.23.2 Summary Table of ANOVA of Sociability scores of Inter-University female players of six games

Source of Variation	Sum of Sq.	df	Mean Sum of Sq.	F-value	p-value
Between	688.840	5	137.768	5.184**	0.0001**
Within	7813.280	294	26.576		
Total	8502.120	299			

** Significant at 0.01 level.

As per the table 4.23.2, F value of 5.184 was found to be significant at 0.01 level of confidence. It means that there were significant differences in the mean scores of Sociability among the players of six games of Inter-University level competition. Now in order to know in which two games significant differences existed, post hoc Analysis of Variance was applied to the mean scores of Sociability of six games players. Baseball players were compared with the players of Football, Handball, Judo, Taekwondo and Wrestling. Similarly the players of other games e.g. Football, Handball, Judo, Taekwondo and Wrestling were compared with the players of all other games by comparing two games one by one.

Table 4.23.3 shows the multiple comparisons of the mean scores of Sociability of female players of six games of Inter-University level competition with each other.

Table 4.23.3 Multiple Comparisons of Mean scores of Sociability Trait of Inter-University Female Players of Six Games

(I) Games		Mean Difference (I-J)	Std. Error	Sig.	95% Confidence Interval	
					Lower Bound	Upper Bound
Baseball	Football	-1.80	1.03	0.082	-3.8291	0.2291
	Handball	-1.92	1.03	0.064	-3.9491	0.1091
	Judo	-0.58	1.031	0.574	-2.6091	1.4491
	Taekwondo	2.10*	1.031	0.043*	0.0709	4.1291
	Wrestling	1.48	1.031	0.152	-0.5491	3.5091
Football	Handball	-0.12	1.031	0.907	-2.1491	1.9091
	Judo	1.22	1.031	0.238	-0.8091	3.2491
	Taekwondo	3.90**	1.031	0.0001**	1.8709	5.9291
	Wrestling	3.28**	1.031	0.002**	1.2509	5.3091
Handball	Judo	1.34	1.031	0.195	-0.6891	3.3691
	Taekwondo	4.02**	1.031	0.0001**	1.9909	6.0491
	Wrestling	3.40**	1.031	0.001**	1.3709	5.4291
Judo	Taekwondo	2.68**	1.031	0.010**	0.6509	4.7091
	Wrestling	2.060*	1.031	0.047*	0.0309	4.0891
Taekwondo	Wrestling	-0.62	1.031	0.548	-2.6491	1.4091

* The mean difference is significant at the 0.05 level.
**The mean difference is significant at the 0.01 level

As per the table4.23.3 , significant differences existed between the Baseball and Taekwondo ($p<0.043$), Football and Taekwondo ($p<0.001$), Football and Wrestling ($p<0.002$), Handball with Taekwondo ($p<0.0001$) and Wrestling ($p<0.001$) as well as

Judo with Taekwondo (p<0.010) and Wrestling (p<0.047) and not with players of other games of Inter-University competition. Their mean scores indicate that Baseball players (M=42.74) were better on Sociability than Taekwondo players (M=40.64), Football players (M=44.54) were better than Taekwondo (M=40.64) and wrestlers (M=41.26). Moreover, Handball players (M=44.66) and Judo players (M=43.42) were better than Taekwondo (M=40.64) and Wrestling (M=41.26).

Table 4.24.1 shows the descriptive statistics of the scores of Dominance trait of personality of female sports-persons of Inter-University level competition of six games, i.e. Baseball, Football, Handball, Judo, Taekwondo and Wrestling.

Table 4.24.1 Descriptive Statistics of Dominance Trait of Inter-University female players of six games

Games	N	Mean	Std. Dev.	Std. Error
Baseball	50	40.66	4.434	0.627
Football	50	40.98	4.483	0.634
Handball	50	41.12	3.508	0.496
Judo	50	41.64	4.158	0.588
Taekwondo	50	39.52	4.087	0.577
Wrestling	50	40.52	3.699	0.523
Total	300	40.74	4.096	0.236

As per the above table, the mean and standard deviation scores of Dominance of the players of six games were as Baseball (40.66 ± 4.43), Football (40.98 ± 4.48), Handball (41.12 ± 3.50), Judo (41.64 ± 4.15), Taekwondo (39.52 ± 4.08), and Wrestling (40.52 ± 3.69) respectively.

Table 4.24.2 shows the results of Analysis of Variance of scores of Dominance of female sportspersons who have participated at Inter-University level competition.

Table 4.24.2 Summary Table of ANOVA of Dominance scores of Inter-University female players of six games

Source of Variation	Sum of Sq.	df	Mean Sum of Sq.	F-value	p-value
Between	127.760	5	25.552	1.536	0.178
Within	4889.960	294	16.633		
Total	5017.720	299			

As per the above table, F-value of 1.536 was not found to be statistically significant at 0.05 level which shows that no significant differences existed among the female sports-persons of six games who have participated at Inter-University level of competition. So there is no need to apply the post-hoc Analysis of Variance technique on the scores of Dominance of six games of Inter-University level female players.

Table 4.25.1 shows the descriptive statistics of the scores of Extraversion trait of personality of female sports-persons of Inter-University level competition of six games, i.e. Baseball, Football, Handball, Judo, Taekwondo and Wrestling.

Table 4.25.1 Descriptive Statistics of Extraversion of Inter-University female players of six games

Games	N	Mean	Std. Dev.	Std. Error
Baseball	50	34.76	5.145	0.727
Football	50	36.96	4.856	0.686
Handball	50	37.02	4.709	0.666
Judo	50	36.20	4.472	0.632
Taekwondo	50	34.28	4.660	0.659
Wrestling	50	35.12	3.461	0.489
Total	300	35.72	4.666	0.269

As per the table 4.25.1, the mean and standard deviation scores of Extraversion of the players of six games were as Baseball (34.76 ± 5.14), Football (36.96 ± 4.85), Handball (37.02 ± 4.70), Judo (36.20 ± 4.47), Taekwondo (34.28 ± 4.66) and Wrestling (35.12 ± 3.46) respectively.

Table 4.25.2 shows the results of Analysis of Variance of scores of Extraversion Trait of female sportspersons who have participated at Inter-University level competition.

Table 4.25.2 Summary Table of ANOVA of Extraversion scores of Inter-University female players of six games

Source of Variation	Sum of Sq.	df	Mean Sum of Sq.	F-value	p-value
Between	340.657	5	68.131	3.246**	0.007**
Within	6171.380	294	20.991		
Total	6512.037	299			

** Significant at 0.01 level of confidence

As per the above table, F value of 3.246 was found to be significant at 0.01 level of confidence. It means that there were significant differences in the mean scores of Extraversion among the players of six games of Inter-University level competition. Now in order to know in which two games significant differences existed, post hoc Analysis of Variance was applied to the mean scores of Extraversion of six games players. Baseball players were compared with the players of Football, Handball, Judo, Taekwondo and Wrestling. Similarly the players of other games e.g. Football, Handball, Judo, Taekwondo and Wrestling were compared with the players of all other games by comparing two games one by one.

Table 4.25.3 shows the multiple comparisons of the mean scores of Extraversion Trait of female players of six games of Inter-University level competition with each other.

Table 4.25.3 Multiple Comparisons of Mean scores of Extraversion of Inter-University Female Players of Six Games

(I) Games		Mean Difference (I-J)	Std. Error	Sig.	95% Confidence Interval	
					Lower Bound	Upper Bound
Baseball	Football	-2.20*	0.916	0.017*	-4.0034	-0.3966
	Handball	-2.26*	0.916	0.014*	-4.0634	-0.4566
	Judo	-1.44	0.916	0.117	-3.2434	0.3634
	Taekwondo	0.48	0.916	0.601	-1.3234	2.2834
	Wrestling	-0.36	0.916	0.695	-2.1634	1.4434
Football	Handball	-0.06	0.916	0.948	-1.8634	1.7434
	Judo	0.76	0.916	0.408	-1.0434	2.5634
	Taekwondo	2.68**	0.916	0.004**	0.8766	4.4834
	Wrestling	1.84*	0.916	0.046*	0.0366	3.6434
Handball	Judo	0.82	0.916	0.372	-0.9834	2.6234
	Taekwondo	2.74**	0.916	0.003**	0.9366	4.5434
	Wrestling	1.90*	0.916	0.039*	0.0966	3.7034
Judo	Taekwondo	1.92*	0.916	0.037*	0.1166	3.7234
	Wrestling	1.08	0.916	0.239	-0.7234	2.8834
Taekwondo	Wrestling	-0.84	0.916	0.360	-2.6434	0.9634

* The mean difference is significant at the 0.05 level.
** The mean difference is significant at the 0.01 level.

As per the above table, significant differences existed between the Baseball and Football ($p<0.017$) and Handball ($p<0.014$), Football and Taekwondo($p<0.004$), and

Wrestling (p,0.046), Handball with Taekwondo(p<0.003),& Wrestling(p<0.039) as well as Judo with Taekwondo (0.037) and not with players of other games of Inter-University competition. Their mean scores indicate that Football players (M=36.96) and Handball players (M=37.02) were better on Extraversion than Baseball players (M=34.76), Football players (M=36.96) were better than Taekwondo (M=34.28) and wrestlers (M=35.12). Moreover, Handball players (M=37.02) were better than Taekwondo (M=34.28) and Wrestling (M=35.12). Judo (M=36.20) were better than Taekwondo players (M=34.28).

Table 4.26.1 shows the descriptive statistics of the scores of Conventionality trait of personality of female sports-persons of Inter-University level competition of six games, i.e. Baseball, Football, Handball, Judo, Taekwondo and Wrestling.

Table 2.26.1 Descriptive Statistics of Conventionality of Inter-University female players of six games

Games	N	Mean	Std. Dev.	Std. Error
Baseball	50	35.34	4.470	0.632
Football	50	36.58	4.426	0.626
Handball	50	36.68	3.976	0.562
Judo	50	36.46	3.632	0.513
Taekwondo	50	34.04	3.625	0.512
Wrestling	50	35.18	3.810	0.538
Total	300	35.71	4.084	0.235

As per the above table, the mean and standard deviation scores of Conventionality of the players of six games were as Baseball (35.34 ± 4.47), Football (36.58 ± 4.42), Handball (36.68 ± 3.97), Judo (36.46 ± 3.63), Taekwondo (34.04 ± 3.62) and Wrestling (35.18 ± 3.81).

Table 4.26.2 shows the results of Analysis of Variance of scores of Conventionality of female sportspersons who have participated at Inter-University level competition.

Table 4.26.2 Summary Table of ANOVA of Conventionality scores of Inter-University female players of six games

Source of Variation	Sum of Sq.	df	Mean Sum of Sq.	F-value	p-value
Between	273.347	5	54.669	3.408**	0.005**
Within	4716.000	294	16.041		
Total	4989.347	299			

** Significant at 0.01 level of confidence

As per the above table, F value of 3.408 was found to be significant at 0.01 level of confidence. It means that there were significant differences in the mean scores of Conventionality among the players of six games of Inter-University level competition. Now in order to know in which two games significant differences existed, post hoc Analysis of Variance was applied to the mean scores of Conventionality of six games players. Baseball players were compared with the players of Football, Handball, Judo, Taekwondo and Wrestling. Similarly the players of other games e.g. Football, Handball, Judo, Taekwondo and Wrestling were compared with the players of all other games by comparing two games one by one.

Table 4.26.3 shows the multiple comparisons of the mean scores of Conventionality of female players of six games of Inter-University level competition with each other.

Table 4.26.3 Multiple Comparisons of Mean scores of Conventionality Trait of Inter-University Female Players of Six Games

(I) Games		Mean Difference (I-J)	Std. Error	Sig.	95% Confidence Interval	
					Lower Bound	Upper Bound
Baseball	Football	-1.24	0.801	0.123	-2.8165	0.3365
	Handball	-1.34	0.801	0.095	-2.9165	0.2365
	Judo	-1.12	0.801	0.163	-2.6965	0.4565
	Taekwondo	1.30	0.801	0.106	-0.2765	2.8765
	Wrestling	0.16	0.801	0.842	-1.4165	1.7365
Football	Handball	-0.10	0.801	0.901	-1.6765	1.4765
	Judo	0.12	0.801	0.881	-1.4565	1.6965
	Taekwondo	2.54**	0.801	0.002**	0.9635	4.1165
	Wrestling	1.40	0.801	0.082	-0.1765	2.9765
Handball	Judo	0.22	0.801	0.784	-1.3565	1.7965
	Taekwondo	2.64**	0.801	0.001**	1.0635	4.2165
	Wrestling	1.50	0.801	0.062	-0.0765	3.0765
Judo	Taekwondo	2.42**	0.801	0.003**	0.8435	3.9965
	Wrestling	1.28	0.801	0.111	-0.2965	2.8565
Taekwondo	Wrestling	-1.14	0.801	0.156	-2.7165	0.4365

* The mean difference is significant at the 0.05 level.
** The mean difference is significant at the 0.01 level.

As per the above table, significant differences existed between Football and Taekwondo ($p < 0.002$) and Handball with Taekwondo ($p<0.001$) as well as Judo with

Taekwondo ($p<0.003$) and not with players of other games of Inter-University competition. Their mean scores indicate that Football players (M=36.58) were better on Conventionality trait than Taekwondo players (M=34.04) Handball players (M=36.68) were better than Taekwondo (M=34.04). Moreover Judo (M=36.46) were better than Taekwondo players (M=34.04).

Table 4.27.1 shows the descriptive statistics of the scores of Self-Concept trait of personality of female sports-persons of Inter-University level competition of six games, i.e. Baseball, Football, Handball, Judo, Taekwondo and Wrestling.

Table 4.27.1 Descriptive Statistics of Self-Concept Trait of Inter-University female players of six games

Games	N	Mean	Std. Dev.	Std. Error
Baseball	50	39.58	5.111	0.722
Football	50	39.48	4.849	0.685
Handball	50	40.16	4.735	0.669
Judo	50	39.36	5.224	0.738
Taekwondo	50	37.46	4.459	0.630
Wrestling	50	38.50	4.267	0.603
Total	300	39.09	4.826	0.278

As per the above table, the means and standard deviation scores of Self-Concept of the players of six games were as Baseball (39.58 ± 5.11), Football (39.48 ± 4.48), Handball (40.16 ± 4.73), Judo (39.36 ± 5.22), Taekwondo (37.46 ± 4.45) and Wrestling (38.50 ± 4.26) respectively.

Table 4.27.2 shows the results of Analysis of Variance of scores of Self-Concept Trait of female sportspersons who have participated at Inter-University level competition.

Table 4.27.2 Summary Table of ANOVA of Self-Concept scores of Inter- University female players of six games

Source of Variation	Sum of Sq.	df	Mean Sum of Sq.	F-value	p-value
Between	230.750	5	46.150	2.014	0.077
Within	6735.820	294	22.911		
Total	6966.570	299			

As per the above table, F-value of 2.014 was not found to be statistically significant at 0.05 level which shows that no significant differences existed on Self-Concept trait among the female sports-persons of six games who have participated at Inter-University level of competition. So there was no need to apply the post-hoc Analysis of Variance technique on the scores of Self-Concept of six games of Inter-University level female players.

Table 4.28.1 shows the descriptive statistics of the scores of Mental Toughness trait of personality of female sports-persons of Inter-University level competition of six games, i.e. Baseball, Football, Handball, Judo, Taekwondo and Wrestling.

Table 4.28.1 Descriptive Statistics of Mental Toughness Trait of Inter-University Female players of six games

Games	N	Mean	Std. Dev.	Std. Error
Baseball	50	39.10	4.408	0.623
Football	50	40.38	4.384	0.620
Handball	50	41.72	4.281	0.6054
Judo	50	40.08	3.827	0.541
Taekwondo	50	38.50	3.813	0.539
Wrestling	50	39.24	3.2611	0.461
Total	300	39.83	4.119	0.237

As per the above table, the mean and standard deviation scores of Mental Toughness of the players of six games were as Baseball (39.10 ± 4.40), Football (40.38 ± 4.38), Handball (41.72 ± 4.28), Judo (40.08 ± 3.82), Taekwondo (38.50 ± 3.81) and Wrestling (39.24 ± 3.26) respectively.

Table 4.28.2 shows the results of Analysis of Variance of scores of Mental Toughness Trait of female sportspersons who have participated at Inter-University level competition.

Table 4.28.2 Summary Table of ANOVA of Mental Toughness scores of Inter-University female players of six games

Source of Variation	Sum of Sq.	df	Mean Sum of Sq.	F-value	p-value
Between	329.337	5	65.867	4.082**	0.001**
Within	4743.660	294	16.135		
Total	5072.997	299			

** Significant at 0.01 level of confidence

As per the above table, F value of 4.082 was found to be significant at 0.01 level of confidence. It means that there were significant differences in the mean scores of Mental Toughness Trait among the players of six games of Inter-University level competition. Now in order to know in which two games significant differences existed, post hoc Analysis of Variance was applied to the mean scores of Mental Toughness Trait of six games players. Baseball players were compared with the players of Football, Handball, Judo, Taekwondo and Wrestling. Similarly the players of other games e.g. Football, Handball, Judo, Taekwondo and Wrestling were compared with the players of all other games by comparing two games one by one.

Table 4.28.3 shows the multiple comparisons of the mean scores of Mental Toughness Trait of female players of six games of Inter-University level competition with each other.

Table 4.28.3 Multiple Comparisons of Mean scores of Mental Toughness of Inter-University Female Players of Six Games

(I) Games		Mean Difference (I-J)	Std. Error	Sig.	95% Confidence Interval	
					Lower Bound	Upper Bound
Baseball	Football	-1.28	0.803	0.112	-2.8611	0.3011
	Handball	-2.62*	0.803	0.001**	-4.2011	-1.0389
	Judo	-0.98	0.803	0.223	-2.5611	0.6011
	Taekwondo	0.60	0.803	0.456	-0.9811	2.1811
	Wrestling	-0.14	0.803	0.862	-1.7211	1.4411
Football	Handball	-1.34	0.803	0.096	-2.9211	0.2411
	Judo	0.30	0.803	0.709	-1.2811	1.8811
	Taekwondo	1.88*	0.803	0.020*	0.2989	3.4611
	Wrestling	1.14	0.803	0.157	-0.4411	2.7211
Handball	Judo	1.64*	0.803	0.042*	0.0589	3.2211
	Taekwondo	3.22*	0.803	0.0001**	1.6389	4.8011
	Wrestling	2.48*	0.803	0.002**	0.8989	4.0611
Judo	Taekwondo	1.58	0.803	0.050*	-0.0011	3.1611
	Wrestling	0.84	0.803	0.297	-0.7411	2.4211
Taekwondo	Wrestling	-0.74	0.803	0.358	-2.3211	0.8411

* The mean difference is significant at the 0.05 level.

** The mean difference is significant at the 0.01 level.

As per the above table, significant differences existed between the Baseball and Handball ($p<0.001$), Football and Taekwondo ($p<0.020$), Handball with Judo ($p<0.042$),

Taekwondo ($p<0.001$) and Wrestling ($p<0.002$) as well as Judo with Taekwondo (0.050) and not with players of other games of Inter-University competition. Their mean scores indicate that Handball players (M=41.72) were better on Mental Toughness than Baseball (M=39.10), Judo (M=40.08), Taekwondo (M=38.50) and Wrestling players (M=39.24). Football players (M=40.38) were better than Taekwondo (M=38.50). But Judo players (M=40.08) were better than Taekwondo players (M=38.50).

Table 4.29.1 shows the descriptive statistics of the scores of Emotional Stability trait of personality of female sports-persons of Inter-University level competition of six games i.e. Baseball, Football, Handball, Judo, Taekwondo and Wrestling.

Table 4.29.1 Descriptive Statistics of Emotional Stability Trait of Inter-University Female players of six games

Games	N	Mean	Std. Dev.	Std. Error
Baseball	50	40.32	5.195	0.734
Football	50	40.70	4.982	0.704
Handball	50	40.74	5.777	0.817
Judo	50	41.80	4.598	0.650
Taekwondo	50	38.72	4.361	0.616
Wrestling	50	40.60	4.015	0.567
Total	300	40.48	4.901	0.282

As per the above table, the means and standard deviation scores of Emotional Stability of the players of six games were as Baseball (40.32 ± 5.19), Football (40.70 ± 4.98), Handball (40.74 ± 5.77), Judo (41.80 ± 4.59), Taekwondo (38.72 ± 4.36) and Wrestling (40.60 ± 4.01).

Table 4.29.2 shows the results of Analysis of Variance of scores of Emotional Stability Trait of female sportspersons who have participated at Inter-University level competition.

Table 4.29.2 Summary Table of ANOVA of Emotional Stability Trait scores of Inter-University female players of six games

Source of Variation	**Sum of Sq.**	**df**	**Mean Sum of Sq.**	**F-value**	**p-value**
Between	249.800	5	49.960	2.119	0.063
Within	6933.080	294	23.582		
Total	7182.880	299			

As per the above table, F-value of 2.119 was not found to be statistically significant at 0.05 level which shows that no significant differences existed on Emotional Stability Trait among the female sports-persons of six games who have participated at Inter-University level of competition. So there was no need to apply the post-hoc Analysis of Variance technique on the scores of Emotional Stability of six games of Inter-University level female players.

Table 4.30.1 shows the descriptive statistics of the scores of Internal locus of control trait of personality of female sports-persons of Inter-University level competition of six games i.e. Baseball, Football, Handball, Judo, Taekwondo and Wrestling.

Table 4.30.1 Descriptive Statistics of Internal Locus of Control of Inter-University Female players of six games

Games	N	Mean	Std. Dev.	Std. Error
Baseball	50	10.42	4.281	0.605
Football	50	9.70	5.406	0.764
Handball	50	8.74	4.839	0.684
Judo	50	9.50	4.305	0.608
Taekwondo	50	12.06	3.328	0.470
Wrestling	50	9.10	3.903	0.551
Total	300	9.92	4.491	0.259

As per the above table, the mean and standard deviation scores of Internal locus of control of the players of six games were as Baseball (10.42 ± 4.28), Football (9.70 ± 5.40), Handball (8.74 ± 4.83), Judo (9.50 ± 4.30), Taekwondo (12.06 ± 3.32) and Wrestling (9.10 ± 3.90) respectively.

Table 4.30.2 shows the results of Analysis of Variance of scores of Internal Locus of control of female sportspersons who have participated at Inter-University level competition.

Table 4.30.2 Summary Table of ANOVA of Internal LOC scores of Inter-University Females players of six games

Games	Sum of Sq.	Df	Mean Sum of Sq.	F-value	p-value
Between	355.960	5	71.192	3.687**	0.003**
Within	5676.120	294	19.307		
Total	6032.080	299			

** Significant at 0.01 level.

As per the above table, F value of 3.687 was found to be significant at 0.01 level of confidence. It means that there were significant differences in the mean scores of Internal locus of control among the players of six games of Inter-University level competition. Now in order to know in which two games significant differences existed, Post hoc Analysis of Variance was applied to the mean scores of Internal LOC of six games players. Baseball players were compared with the players of Football, Handball, Judo, Taekwondo and Wrestling. Similarly the players of other games e.g. Football, Handball, Judo, Taekwondo and Wrestling were compared with the players of all other games by comparing two games one by one.

Table 4.30.3 shows the multiple comparisons of the mean scores of Internal locus of control of female players of six games of Inter-University level competition with each other.

Table 4.30.3. Multiple Comparisons of Mean scores of Internal LOC of Inter-University Female Players of Six Games

(I) Games		Mean Difference (I-J)	Std. Error	Sig.	95% Confidence Interval	
					Lower Bound	Upper Bound
Baseball	Football	0.72	0.878	0.413	-1.0095	2.4495
	Handball	1.68*	0.878	0.057*	-0.0495	3.4095
	Judo	0.92	0.878	0.296	-0.8095	2.6495
	Taekwondo	-1.64	0.878	0.063	-3.3695	0.0895
	Wrestling	1.32	0.878	0.134	-0.4095	3.0495
Football	Handball	0.96	0.878	0.276	-0.7695	2.6895
	Judo	0.20	0.878	0.820	-1.5295	1.9295
	Taekwondo	-2.36**	0.878	0.008**	-4.0895	-0.6305
	Wrestling	0.60	0.878	0.495	-1.1295	2.3295
Handball	Judo	-0.76	0.878	0.388	-2.4895	0.9695
	Taekwondo	-3.32**	0.878	0.0001**	-5.0495	-1.5905
	Wrestling	-0.36	0.878	0.682	-2.0895	1.3695
Judo	Taekwondo	-2.56**	0.878	0.004**	-4.2895	-0.8305
	Wrestling	0.40	0.878	0.649	-1.3295	2.1295
Taekwondo	Wrestling	2.96**	0.878	0.001**	1.2305	4.6895

* The mean difference is significant at the 0.05 level.
** The mean difference is significant at the 0.01 level.

As per the above table, significant differences existed between the Baseball and Handball ($p < 0.05$), Football and Taekwondo ($p<0.008$), Handball with Taekwondo (p<0.001) as well as Judo with Taekwondo (p<0.004) and Taekwondo and Wrestling (p<0.001) but not with players of other games of Inter-University competition. Their mean scores indicate that Baseball players (M=10.42) were better on Internal LOC than Handball players (M=8.74), Taekwondo players (M=12.06) were better than Football players (M=9.70), Handball players (M=8.74), Judo (M=9.50) and Wrestling players (M=9.10).

Table 4.31.1 shows the descriptive statistics of the scores of External locus of control trait of personality of female sports-persons of Inter-University level competition of six games, i.e. Baseball, Football, Handball, Judo, Taekwondo and Wrestling.

Table 4.31.1. Descriptive Statistics of External LOC of Inter-University Female players of six games

Games	N	Mean	Std. Dev.	Std. Error
Baseball	50	23.42	4.844	0.685
Football	50	21.50	5.817	0.822
Handball	50	18.72	6.452	0.912
Judo	50	23.44	5.855	0.828
Taekwondo	50	22.72	3.608	0.510
Wrestling	50	25.88	5.216	0.737
Total	300	22.61	5.760	0.332

As per the above table, the mean and standard deviation scores of Internal locus of control of the players of six games were as Baseball (23.42 ±4.84), Football (21.50±5.81), Handball (18.72±6.45), Judo (23.44±5.85), Taekwondo (22.72±3.60) and Wrestling (25.88±5.21) respectively.

Table 4.31.2 shows the results of Analysis of Variance of scores of External Locus of control of female sports-persons who have participated at Inter-University level competition.

Table 4.31.2 Summary Table of ANOVA of External LOC scores of Inter-University female players of six games

Source of Variation	Sum of Sq.	df	Mean Sum of Sq.	F-value	p-value
Between	1420.707	5	284.141	9.827**	0.0001**
Within	8500.440	294	28.913		
Total	9921.147	299			

** Significant at 0.01 level.

As per the above table, F value of 9.827 was found to be significant at 0.001 level of confidence. It means that there were significant differences in the mean scores of External locus of control among the players of six games of Inter-University level competition. Now in order to know in which two games significant differences existed, post hoc Analysis of Variance was applied to the mean scores of External LOC of six games players. Baseball players were compared with the players of Football, Handball, Judo, Taekwondo and Wrestling. Similarly the players of other games e.g. Football, Handball, Judo, Taekwondo and Wrestling were compared with the players of all other games by comparing two games one by one.

Table 4.31.3 shows the multiple comparisons of the mean scores of External locus of control of female players of six games of Inter-University level competition with each other.

Table 4.31.3. Multiple Comparisons of Mean scores of External LOC of Inter-University Female Players of Six Games

(I) Games		Mean Difference (I-J)	Std. Error	Sig.	95% Confidence Interval	
					Lower Bound	Upper Bound
Baseball	Football	1.92	1.075	0.075	-0.1965	4.0365
	Handball	4.7**	1.075	0.0001**	2.5835	6.8165
	Judo	-0.02	1.075	0.985	-2.1365	2.0965
	Taekwondo	0.70	1.075	0.516	-1.4165	2.8165
	Wrestling	-2.46*	1.075	0.023*	-4.5765	-0.3435
Football	Handball	2.78**	1.075	0.010**	0.6635	4.8965
	Judo	-1.94	1.075	0.072	-4.0565	0.1765
	Taekwondo	-1.22	1.075	0.258	-3.3365	0.8965
	Wrestling	-4.38**	1.075	0.0001**	-6.4965	-2.2635
Handball	Judo	-4.72**	1.075	0.0001**	-6.8365	-2.6035
	Taekwondo	-4.0**	1.075	0.0001**	-6.1165	-1.8835
	Wrestling	-7.16**	1.075	0.0001**	-9.2765	-5.0435
Judo	Taekwondo	0.72	1.075	0.504	-1.3965	2.8365
	Wrestling	-2.44*	1.075	0.024*	-4.5565	-0.3235
Taekwondo	Wrestling	-3.16**	1.075	0.004**	-5.2765	-1.0435

* The mean difference is significant at the 0.05 level
** The mean difference is significant at 0.01 level.

As per the table4.31.3, significant differences existed between the Baseball with Handball ($p<0.001$) and Wrestling ($p<0.023$), Football with Handball ($p<0.010$),

Wrestling ($p<0.001$) and Handball with Judo ($p<0.001$), Taekwondo ($p<0.001$) and Wrestling ($p<0.001$) as well as Judo with Wrestling ($p<0.024$) and Taekwondo with Wrestling ($p<0.004$) and not with players of other games of Inter-University competition. Their mean scores indicate that Baseball players (M=23.42) were better on External locus of control trait than Handball players (M=18.72) but Wrestlers (M=25.88) were better than Baseball (M=23.42), Football (M=21.50), Handball (M=18.72), Judo (M=23.44) and Taekwondo players (M= 22.72). Football players (M=21.50) were better than Handball players (M=18.72). Moreover, Judo (M= 23.44) and Taekwondo players (M=22.72) were better than Handball players (M=18.72).

4.6 RELATIONSHIP BETWEEN DIFFERENT COMPONENTS OF PERSONALITY CHARACTERISTICS OF FEMALE SPORTSPERSONS

One of the objectives of the present study was to establish relationship among the different components of all the personality characteristics, i.e. Sociability, Dominance, Extraversion, Conventionality, Self-Concept, Mental Toughness and Emotional Stability as well as Internal and External locus of control of female sports-persons who participated at Inter-College and Inter-University level competition. For this purpose, co-efficient of correlation were calculated with the help of Pearson's product moment method for the total sample, and then for the Inter-College sportspersons and Inter-University sportspersons separately. These results are given in the following tables.

Table 4.32 shows the co-efficient of correlation among the seven personality characteristics along with the Internal and External locus of control of female sports-persons of both Inter-College and Inter-University level competition combined.

Table 4.32 Co-efficient of correlations among all the personality characteristics of Female Sports-persons

Traits	Sociability	Dominance	Extraversion	Conventionality	Self Concept	Mental Toughness	Emotional Stability	Internal LOC	External LOC
Sociability	1	0.423^{**}	0.616^{**}	0.496^{**}	0.652^{**}	0.485^{**}	0.465^{**}	-0.286^{**}	-0.087^{*}
Dominance		1	0.414^{**}	0.397^{**}	0.433^{**}	0.273^{**}	0.301^{**}	-0.062	-0.129^{*}
Extraversion			1	0.447^{**}	0.573^{**}	0.518^{**}	0.405^{**}	-0.198^{**}	-0.146^{**}
Conventionality				1	0.520^{**}	0.359^{**}	0.362^{**}	-0.103^{*}	-0.087^{*}
Self Concept					1	0.471^{**}	0.430^{**}	-0.215^{**}	-0.052
Mental Toughness						1	0.320^{**}	-0.116^{**}	-0.138^{**}
Emotional Stability							1	-0.164^{**}	-0.016
Internal LOC								1	-0.174^{**}
External LOC									1

* Correlation is significant at the 0.05 level (2-tailed).
** Correlation is significant at the 0.01 level (2-tailed).

As per the table4.32, it has been found that all the seven traits of personality have positive and significant relationship with each other, e.g. Sociability has a correlation coefficients ranged from 0.423 (Dominance) and 0.652 (Self-Concept). Dominance has the highest correlation with Self-Concept (r=0.433) and lowest with Mental Toughness (r=0.273). Extraversion has higher correlation co-efficient with Self-Concept (r=0,573) and lowest with Emotional Stability (r=0.405) Conventionality has the maximum correlation with Self-Concept (r=0.520) and the minimum with Mental Toughness (r=0.359). Self-Concept has positive co-efficient of correlation with Mental Toughness (r=0.471) and Emotional Stability (r=0.430), where as Mental Toughness has r= 0.320 with Emotional Stability. All these co-efficient of correlation were significant at 0.01 level.

But in case of correlations between these seven personality traits and Internal and External locus of control are concerned, it has been found that co-efficient of correlation were negative and low and in some cases non significant. For example, Sociability has negative and low correlation with Internal LOC (r=-0.286) and External locus of control (r=-0.087 NS). Dominance has negative, and low relationship (r=-0.062 NS) with Internal and r=-0.129 with External LOC. Extraversion and Conventionality again had negative and low correlation with Internal (-0.198 & -0.103) and External LOC (r= -0.146 & -0.087 NS). Similarly Self-Concept, Mental Toughness and Emotional Stability had negative and low correlation co-efficient with Internal (r= -0.215, -0.116 & -0.164) and External LOC (r= -0.052 NS, -0.138 & -0. 016 NS) respectively. But Internal LOC has also a negative and low correlation with External LOC (r=-0.174).

Table 4.33 shows the co-efficient of correlation among the seven personality characteristics along with the Internal and External locus of control of female sports-persons of both Inter-College level competitions only.

Table 4.33 Co-efficient of correlation among all the personality characteristics of Inter-College Female Sports-persons

Trait	Sociability	Dominance	Extraversion	Conventionality	Self Concept	Mental Toughness	Emotional Stability	Internal LOC	External LOC
Sociability	1	0.486^{**}	0.681^{**}	0.541^{**}	0.729^{**}	0.567^{**}	0.502^{**}	-0.213^{**}	-0.077
Dominance		1	0.491^{**}	0.438^{**}	0.487^{**}	0.434^{**}	0.371^{**}	0.032	-0.169^{**}
Extraversion			1	0.540^{**}	0.665^{**}	0.603^{**}	0.461^{**}	-0.130^{*}	-0.105
Convention				1	0.566^{**}	0.453^{**}	0.448^{**}	0.006	-0.125^{*}
Self Concept					1	0.587^{**}	0.520^{**}	-0.192^{**}	-0.064
Mental Toughness						1	0.425^{**}	-0.088	-0.105
Emotional Stability							1	-0.080	-0.083
Internal LOC								1	-0.250^{**}
External LOC									1

* Correlation is significant at 0.05 level
**Correlation is significant at the 0.01 level (2-tailed)

As per the table 4.33, the same results were observed in case of female sportspersons of Inter-College level competition in the correlations of seven traits of personality traits as well as Internal and External locus of control variables. There were positive and significant correlations among the seven personality characteristics. As it has been noticed that Sociability has the highest correlation co-efficient with Self-Concept (r=0.729) and the lowest was with Dominance (r=0.486). Dominance has the maximum correlation with Extraversion (r=0. 491) and the minimum with Emotional Stability (r= 0,371), Extraversion has the highest co-efficient was with Self-Concept (r=0.665) and the lowest with Emotional Stability (r=0. 461). Conventionality correlation ranged from Emotional Stability (r=0.448) and Self-Concept (r=0.566). Self concept has r=0.587 with Mental Toughness and r= 0.520 with Emotional Stability. Mental Toughness has r= 0.425 with Emotional Stability. All these co-efficient of correlation were significant at 0.01 level.

But in case of correlations between these seven personality traits and Internal and External locus of control were concerned, it has been found that co-efficient of correlation were negative and low and in some cases non significant. For example, Sociability has negative and low correlation with Internal LOC (r=-0.213) and External locus of control (r=-0.077 NS). Dominance has negative, low relationship (r=-0.032NS) with Internal and r=-0.169 with External LOC. Extraversion and Conventionality again had negative and low correlation with Internal (-0.130 & 0.006 NS) and External LOC (r= -0.105 NS & -0. 125). Similarly Self-Concept, Mental Toughness and emotional maturity had negative and low correlation co-efficient with Internal (r= -0.192, -0.088 NS & -0.080 NS) and External LOC (r= -.064 NS, -0.105 NS & -0. 083 NS) respectively. But Internal LOC has also a negative and low correlation with External LOC (r=-0. 250).

Table 4.34 shows the cc-efficient of correlation among the seven personality characteristics along with the Internal and External locus of control of female sports-persons of Inter-University level competition only.

Table 4.34 Co-efficient of correlation among all the personality characteristics of Inter-University Female Sports-persons

Traits	Sociability	Dominance	Extraversion	Conventionality	Self Concept	Mental Toughness	Emotional Stability	Internal LOC	External LOC
Sociability	1	0.344**	0.526**	0.443**	0.555**	0.363**	0.414**	-0.381**	-0.117*
Dominance		1	0.321**	0.350**	0.371**	0.065	0.219**	-0.171**	-0.084
Extraversion			1	0.334**	0.459**	0.398**	0.332**	-0.283**	-0.219**
Conventionality				1	0.461**	0.245**	0.263**	-0.243**	-0.026
Self Concept					1	0.327**	0.325**	-0.249**	-0.026
Mental Toughness						1	0.173**	-0.145*	-0.218**
Emotional Stability							1	-0.263**	0.057
Internal LOC								1	-0.059
External LOC									1

* Correlation is significant at the 0.05 level (2-tailed).
**Correlation is significant at the 0.01 level (2-tailed).

As per the table 4.34, the same results were observed when female sportspersons of Inter-University level competition were compared on the basis of the correlations of seven traits of personality traits as well as Internal and External locus of control variables. There were positive and significant correlations among the seven personality characteristics. As it has been noticed that

Sociability has the highest co-efficient with Self-Concept (r=0.555) and the lowest was with Dominance (r=0.344). Dominance has the maximum correlation with Self-Concept (r=0.371) and the minimum with Mental Toughness (r= 0.065 NS). Extraversion has the highest co-efficient with Self-Concept (r=0.459) and the lowest with Emotional Stability (r=0.332). Conventionality has highest correlation with Self-Concept (r=0.461) and lowest with Mental Toughness(r=0.245). Self concept has correlation with Mental Toughness (r=0. 327) and Emotional Stability (r=0.325). Mental Toughness has a correlation with Emotional Stability (r=0.173). All these co-efficient of correlation were significant at 0.01 level.

But in case of correlations between these seven personality traits and Internal and External locus of control were concerned, it has been found that co-efficient of correlation were negative and low and in some cases non significant. For example, Sociability has negative correlation with Internal LOC (r=-0.381) and External locus of control (r=-0.117). Dominance has negative and low relationship (r= -0.171) with Internal and (r=-0.084 NS) with External LOC. Extraversion and Conventionality again had negative and low correlation with Internal (r=-0.283 & -243) and External LOC (r= -0.219 & -0.026NS). Similarly Self-Concept, Mental Toughness and Emotional Stability had negative and low correlation co-efficient with Internal (r= -0.249, -0.145 & -0.263) and External LOC (r= -0.026 NS, -0.218 & -0. 057 NS) respectively. But Internal LOC had also a negative and low correlation with External LOC (r=-0.059 NS).

4.7 RELATIONSHIP OF PERSONALITY CHARACTERISTICS WITH LOCUS OF CONTROL

One of the objectives of the study was to find out the differences on seven different personality characteristics, i.e Sociability, Dominance, Extraversion, Self-Concept, Conventionality, Mental Toughness and Emotional Stability between the female sports-persons with Internal and External locus of control. For this purpose, the total sample was divided into two groups on the basis of their scores on locus of control with the criterion of median scores. The median score was 35 on both intra-college and intra-university female athletes. It means that those who obtained score more than 35 were included in the group of Internal locus of control and those who got scores less than 35 formed the External locus of control group. In this way, 327 out of 600 female sports-persons were found to be in the group of Internal locus of control, whereas 273 out of 600 female players were in the External locus of control group. Mean and standard deviations on the scores of seven personality characteristics were calculated and then t-ratios were computed in order to find out if significant differences existed on these personality traits between two groups of female athletes formed on the basis of locus of control variable.

Table 4.35 shows the mean scores differences on the seven personality characteristics between Internal and External locus of control female sports-persons.

TABLE 4.35 Mean and SD and t-ratios of scores of Personality Characteristic of Female Sports-persons with Internal and External LOC

Locus of Control		**N**	**Mean**	**Std. Dev.**	**t-value**	**p-value**
Sociability	Internal	327	43.95	5.90	4.09**	0.0001**
	External	273	42.01	5.63		
Dominance	Internal	327	41.13	4.04	2.07*	0.039*
	External	273	40.41	4.43		
Extraversion	Internal	327	36.63	5.01	4.05**	0.0001**
	External	273	34.98	4.90		
Conventionality	Internal	327	35.86	4.31	1.99*	0.048*
	External	273	35.16	4.27		
Self Concept	Internal	327	39.40	5.08	2.50*	0.013*
	External	273	38.36	5.08		
Mental Toughness	Internal	327	40.63	4.34	2.46*	0.014*
	External	273	39.70	4.85		
Emotional Stability	Internal	327	41.00	5.19	1.26	0.208
	External	273	40.46	5.17		

* Significant at 0.05 level of confidence

** Significant at 0.01 level of confidence.

As per the table 4.35, it has been found that significant differences were found on almost all the personality characteristics except Emotional Stability between the female athletes with Internal and External locus of control, where the t-value of 1.26 was not statistically significant, whereas on all other characteristics, the differences existed significantly either at 0.01 or 0.05 level of confidence,. For example, in case of Sociability ($t=4.09, p<0.01$), Dominance ($t=2.07$, $p<0.039$), Extraversion ($t=4.05$, $p<0.001$), Conventionality ($t=1.99$, $p<0.048$), Self-Concept ($t=2.50$, $p<0.013$), and Mental Toughness ($t=2.46$, $p<0.014$).Their mean scores indicate that the female players with Internal locus of control were better on their personality characteristics than those of External locus of control. Their mean scores can be compared as Sociability (M=43.95 & 42.01), Dominance (M= 41.13 & 40.41), Extraversion (M= 36.63 & 34.98), Conventionality (M=35.86 & 35.16), Self-Concept (M=39.40 & 38.36) and Mental Toughness (M=40.63 & 39.70).

Table 4.36 shows the mean scores differences on the seven personality characteristics between Internal and External locus of control of Inter-College female sports-persons.

TABLE 4.36 Mean and SD and t-ratios of scores of Personality Characteristic of Inter-College Female Sports-persons with Internal and External LOC

Locus of Control		N	Mean	Std. Deviation	t-value	p-value
Sociability	Internal	154	44.09	6.28	2.28*	0.023*
	External	146	42.43	6.31		
Dominance	Internal	154	41.31	3.98	1.82	0.070
	External	146	40.39	4.72		
Extraversion	Internal	154	36.66	5.12	2.09*	0.038*
	External	146	35.38	5.55		
Conventionality	Internal	154	35.78	4.40	1.62	0.106
	External	146	34.94	4.59		
Self Concept	Internal	154	39.24	5.14	1.61	0.109
	External	146	38.25	5.56		
Mental Toughness	Internal	154	40.79	4.57	0.76	0.445
	External	146	40.35	5.44		
Emotional Stability	Internal	154	41.47	5.39	1.46	0.144
	External	146	40.55	5.49		

* Significant 0.05 level of confidence

As per the above table, the results show that significant differences were found only in case of Sociability and Extraversion trait of personality between Internal and External locus of control female athletes of Inter-College level. In case of Sociability, t-value was 2.28 ($p<0.023$) and Extraversion ($t=2.09$, $p< 0.038$), where again female players with Internal locus of control (M=44.09 & 36.66) were found to better than those of External LOC (M=42.43 & 35.38) respectively. On other traits of personality, e.g. Dominance, Conventionality, Self-Concept, Mental Toughness and Emotional Stability, t-values were not statistically significant and hence no significant differences existed.

Table 4.37 shows the mean scores differences on the seven personality characteristics between Internal and External locus of control of Inter-University female sports-persons.

TABLE 4.37. Mean and SD and t-ratios of scores of Personality Characteristic of Inter-University Female Sports-persons with Internal and External LOC

Locus of Control		N	Mean	Std. Dev.	t-value	p-value
Sociability	Internal	173	43.83	5.55	3.77**	0.0001**
	External	127	41.54	4.72		
Dominance	Internal	173	40.97	4.10	1.11	0.267
	External	127	40.43	4.09		
Extraversion	Internal	173	36.60	4.92	3.89**	0.0001**
	External	127	34.53	4.01		
Conventionality	Internal	173	35.93	4.24	1.08	0.283
	External	127	35.42	3.87		
Self Concept	Internal	173	39.54	5.04	1.88	0.061
	External	127	38.48	4.47		
Mental Toughness	Internal	173	40.48	4.12	3.20**	0.001**
	External	127	38.96	3.97		
Emotional Stability	Internal	173	40.57	4.99	0.38	0.704
	External	127	40.35	4.80		

** Significant at 0.01 level of confidence.

As per that above table, it has been found that significant differences existed in case of Sociability($t=3.77$, $p<0.001$), Extraversion ($t=3.89$, $p<0.001$), and Mental

Toughness($t=3.20$, $p< 0.001$) where the female sportspersons of Inter-University level with Internal locus of control were found to be better than those of with External LOC. Their mean scores can be contrasted as Sociability (M=43.83 & 41.54), Extraversion (M=36.60 & 34.53) and Mental Toughness (M=40.48 & 38.96) respectively. On all others traits e.g. Dominance, Conventionality, Self-Concept and Emotional Stability, so significant differences were observed as their t-values were not found to be statistically significant.

To conclude, it may be said that no significant differences were found between Inter-College and Inter-University level female sports-persons on almost all the personality characteristics except Mental Toughness and External locus of control variables. But significant differences were found between ball games and Combat Sports female players of college level competition on all the personality characteristics except Mental Toughness, In case of university level players, differences were observed in favour of Sociability, Conventionality, Self-Concept, Mental Toughness and External locus of control. It was also found that all the seven trait of personality of female players have positive and significant relationships with each other both in case of college and university levels competition. But co-efficient of correlations between seven personality traits and Internal and External locus of control were negative and low and non-significant. It was also found that female athletes with Internal and External locus of control differed on their personality characteristics except Emotional Stability. So relationship has been established between personality traits and locus of control of female sports-persons.

4.8 DISCUSSION

In recent years, there has been an increasing amount of attention to the inter-relationships of personality variables and psychological characteristics with athletic performance. Most of this work has been concerned with delineating personality traits of athletes, differentiating among individuals by sports and level of success etc. Studies of measurement of personality traits of athletes and players are vital, if we are to secure the information needed by sport psychologists and coaches, who are charged with responsibility for selection, counselling and also the training of the athletes for competition. It is assumed that the physical abilities of an individual are linked to his personality makeup, because the environment in which physical abilities are presented (i.e. in games) creates an ideal setting for the development of desirable personality traits such as confidence, sociability, cooperativeness, emotional stability, personal adjustment and extraversion which are very essential for increasing the athletic ability of the players and sportsmen (Singh, 1992). The participation in present time is inspired by various physiological present time sports is influenced by various physio-physiological, psycho-sociological factors. During training, besides good physique and physical fitness of the players, main stress is given on the development of different types of motor skills connected with sports in the game as well as on the techniques and strategies of the game. Usually very little attention has been paid to the psychological components which have been proved to improve to performance at the higher levels of competitions sports. The present study would be undertaken to investigate important psychological components of the sports-persons participating at different levels of competition.

In fact, the major dimension of the study of psychological aspect of sports is concerned with inquiries into the personality of sportsmen and sportswomen. There are numerous theories about the personality of athletes. But only a limited amount of research has been undertaken to support these theories. Several investigators have directed their attention towards an understanding of the relationship between personality and level of performance. Hence one of the well known matters in sports personality we about the relationship between personality and sport participation.

It is reasonably assumed that personality functions as a basis for all types of behavior. The person may or may not be cooperative, may have more or less competitiveness, possesses positive or negative leadership qualities or may be emotionally stable or anxious; it all depends upon his personal make-up. Similarly, the level of adjustment may have the corresponding impact on other aspects of his functioning as a social unit. The same applies to the values which form various predispositions in the individuals to find expressions in their sports behavior.

The physical educators and coaches become interested in psychological studies because of the belief that personality plays a role in the selection and participation in physical activities and sports. Moreover, the involvement in physical education and sports contributes to personal and social adjustment. The development of personality and the achievement of desirable social values have been the objectives of sports and physical education since early times. The findings that the athletes are different from non-athletes may not mean that athletics cause enhanced personality characteristics. It may be that athletics and sports produce the more well-adjusted individuals in society or it helps in removing maladjustment.

From the past, one of the well known matters in Sport Psychology we about the connection between personality and sports performance. Although most sport personality research has focused on the description of personality characteristics in athletes and the influence of personality on sport behavior, the study of the effects of sport participation on personality development and change has also been an important area of research. It seems logical to consider that some personality traits (e.g.; competitiveness, self-confidence) are important in achieving success in sport. Well liked belief is that certain personality traits (e.g.; self-regard, self-discipline) may be developed or improved through sport participation i.e.; participation in games and physical activities enhances psychological and physical development. Both of these issues have been extensively investigated over the last three decades.

Personality assessment has always been an area of interest to psychologists. In recent years, the study of the measurement of the personality traits of athletes has become a popular topic of sports psychology research. One of the goals of this research has been to ascertain the role of the athletes' personality in successful competition. So, the athlete's personality has become important in athletic success. Psychologists have developed methods to measure personality that can help us to understand personality characteristics of the athletes. Many psychologists differentiate between an individual's typical style of behaviour and the situation's effect on behaviour. This contrast between psychological characteristics and behavoiur has been critical in the development of personality research in sports.

In the sphere of sports psychology, the personality research was characterized by a tradition of in between group comparisons, e.g.; athletes were compared with non-athletes, successful athletes with less successful ones, and men athletes with women athletes. Comparisons were also made among athletes representing different sports disciplines. These studies generally served performance prediction and selection goals, whether or not these attempts were very successful is difficult to say, but some studies have attempted to demonstrate an "athletic personality."

As personality is reflective of the entire behavioural dimension of individuals, it has strong bearing not only on athletic performance, but it has a direct link with sports performance. Tutko and Richards (1971) had identified a number of personality characteristics related to high athletic achievements such as drive, intelligence, determination, leadership, aggression, coachability, organization, emotionality, mental toughness, self-confidence, responsibility, trust and conscience development.

Personality of sportspersons which has influenced the performance is affected by many factors like anxiety, will to will, and attitude (Kamlesh, 1982).Whether participants in games and sports develop desirable personality characteristics as a result of their participation or people with inborn qualities take to sports and achieve greater goals is an unresolved question. The present personality test which is proposed to be used in the present study measures traits like sociability, dominance, extraversion, self-concept, conventionality, mental toughness, and emotional stability. Another personality characteristic which needs to be probed for the sports-persons is the L.O.C. The construct of L.O.C. is a personality aspect involving an individual's perceived control over events occurring in her life. People are having internal or external L.O.C. Locus of control refers to a person's opinion about control over life events. Locus of control is the extent to which people think that they are responsible for their behavioural results. It has often been quoted as an important factor in achievement oriented behaviour. Some people feel personally responsible for the things that occur to them. They are labelled internals. People with an internal locus of control tend to believe their behaviour effects results, while those with an external locus of control tend to attribute results to outside powers such as destiny, chance, fortune and other people. They feel that their end results in life are determined by forces out of their control. They are labelled as externals. In the field of sports, sports-persons of internal locus of control are required who have self-belief in their talent, ability and potential. Clearly, most people fall between the two extremes forming a continuous distribution of locus of control beliefs. Locus of control is thought to be relatively enduring dispositional characteristics, although certainly changeable through experience. People have to believe in their own abilities to achieve and be jovial. They need to develop a sense of control. People's locus of control effects how they view the world and how they identify the causes of success or failure in their lives. Internal components mean personal whereas external are situational ones.

The variable of locus of control is of major importance in perceiving the nature of learning processes in different kinds of learning situations. The construct of locus of control, essential part of social learning theory of Rotter (1954) is a personality dimension involving an individual's perceived control over events happening in her life. This idea grew out of Rotter's Social learning theory (1954) which provides the general theoretical background for his inception of the nature and effects of reinforcement and his work on levels of expectancies.

According to this theory, the unit of investigation for the study of personality is the interaction of a person and his meaningful environment and it is the study of learned behaviour. Behaviour as explained by personality theorists have a directional feature and this feature is inferred from the effect of reinforcing conditions. The occurrence of behaviour of an individual is determined not only by the nature or importance of goals or reinforcements but also by the person's expectation that the goals will occur. Thus the three basic forms in Rotter's social learning theory are behavioural potential, expectancy and reinforcement value.

4.9 MEASUREMENT OF PERSONALITY CHARACTERISTICS OF FEMALE SPORTS-PERSONS

The first objective of the study was to measure the personality characteristics of the female sportspersons who had participated at inter-college and inter-university level competition. For this purpose, descriptive statistics were computed like mean, median, mode, SD, skewness and kurtosis of the scores of all the variables under study. From the results of the study, it was concluded that the data were normally distributed, as the values of mean, median and mode were nearer to each other and there was less deviation. While comparing the results with those of the original tests, it was found that the results were quite closer with the values as given in the manual of the test. The values of skewness and kurtosis also proved that data had the normal distribution, both in the case of female sports-persons of inter-college and inter-university level of competition.

4.10 COMPARISON OF PERSONALITY CHARACTERISTICS BETWEEN INTER-COLLEGE AND INTER-UNIVERSITY LEVEL FEMALE SPORT-PERSONS

Another objective of the study was to make comparison between female players of inter-college and inter-university level competition on the personality characteristics like sociability, extraversion, dominance, self-concept, conventionality, mental toughness and emotional stability as well as internal and external locus of control variables. The results of t-values calculated revealed that no significant differences were found between inter-college and inter-university level female sports-persons on almost all the personality characteristics, as the t-values were statistically non-significant, except in the case of mental toughness where the t-value was significant at 0.05 level and also in case of external locus of control, which was significant at 0.01 level. Here the inter college level female athletes were found to be more mentally tough and were more externally oriented as compared to those of inter-university level female players. On the other hand, the inter-college and inter-university level sports-persons did not differ much on all other personality characteristics, and if there were differences, they were very minor and hence they have the same level of personality traits. It has also been found by some other studies that the sports-persons whether they play at school, college or university level participation, have the in-built personality traits which have predisposed them to become good sports-persons. There are many personality traits which are required in order to become good sports-persons. As the tool used for measuring the personality characteristics was the sports specific personality inventory which consists of those traits of personality which should be inherent in athletes, e.g.; sociability, extraversion, dominance, self-concept, conventionality, mental toughness and emotional stability. Without these traits of personality, they could not think of participating in sports at any level. Hence the hypothesis of the study that there would be significant differences on personality characteristics between the inter-college and inter-university level female sports-persons was rejected by the findings of this study.

While considering the differences on personality characteristics between inter-college and inter-university level female sports-persons game wise, it was found that in case of baseball game, t-ratios were not statistically significant on all the personality characteristics indicating that no differences were observed and hence all the female sports-persons whether they play at inter-college or inter-university level competition have the same level of personality traits. But in case of football game, significant differences were found only in case of conventionality and self-concept, where the inter university level female athletes were having better level of conventionality and self-concept than inter college level counterparts, as their mean scores were higher than that of inter college level But in case of external locus of control variable, inter college level players were found to be more externally oriented than inter university level players. As experience of participation in sports as well as exposure to sports environment setting helps them to acquire better conventionality and self-concept and also they become less externally oriented and they develop more self-belief and self-sufficiency in sports participation.

Among the inter-college and inter-university female players of handball game, showed that significant differences existed in almost all the personality characteristics except emotional stability, where t-value was statistically not significant, but in all other traits of personality, t-values were found to be significant at either 0.01 or 0.05 level of confidence. The mean scores indicate that the inter university level female sports-persons were better on sociability, dominance, extraversion, conventionality, self-concept and mental toughness than inter college level female players. But on the other hand inter college level female athletes proved to be more internally and externally oriented as compared to the inter university level players. Due to more participation in different level of competition, the players get more experience and become more mature in their game skills; there may be some changes and development in the different traits of personality, which was quite obvious in the case of inter university level female athletes. Of course, in this game, the hypothesis of the study that there would be significant differences on different personality characteristics between female sports-persons of inter-college and inter-university levels competition has been accepted.

So far as the individual sports are concerned, significant differences were not found in case of inter-college and inter-university level female players of judo on almost all the personality characteristics except the second trait of personality, i.e.; dominance where t-ratio was significant statistically and where the inter college level players were getting higher mean scores than the inter university level players and hence inter college levels players were more dominant than inter university level female players, whereas on all other traits of personality, the inter college and inter university level players were having the same level of personality characteristics. Here the hypothesis has been rejected.

But in case of Taekwondo, significant differences were observed on sociability, dominance, extraversion, mental toughness and emotional stability as well as on internal locus of control; but not in favor of conventionality, self-concept and external locus of control. Here again the inter college level female players were getting higher mean scores as compared to inter university level counterparts. But on internal LOC inter university players proved to be more internally oriented. In case of wrestling ,inter college and inter university level female athletes differed on only sociability and internal LOC and not in all other personality characteristics. Here again inter college level players got higher mean score on sociability than inter university level players, whereas inter university level players were found to be more internally oriented than inter college level players. Of course, Gurdev and Nishan (2009) found that the inter-university level cycling riders were significantly better than the inter-college cycling riders and the inter-district cycling riders. But, according to Dalbara and Agyajit (2015), school levels male and female sports-persons did not differ on all personality traits; college level players differed on sociability and university level players on sociability, extraversion, mental toughness and emotional maturity. Surjit & Singh (2015) found that school level athletes were having differences on the external LOC and not on internal, whereas college level athletes and non-athletes did not differ either on external or internal LOC.

4.11 COMPARISON BETWEEN BALL GAMES AND COMBAT SPORTS ON PERSONALITY CHARACTERISTICS

One of the objectives of the study is to find out the differences in all seven characteristics of personality as well as internal and external L.O.C. between the female sportspersons of ball games and combat sports. The ball game players consisted of the games of baseball, football and handball; whereas combat sports players were from judo, taekwondo and wrestling. All the ball games players were team games players, whereas combat sports players were from individual sports. So comparison has been made between individual sports and team game players on all the personality characteristics.

The results of the study indicated that on the total sample, significant differences were found between the female sports-persons of ball games and combat sports in favour of dominance and emotional stability, but not in case of all other personality characteristics. Here the combat sports female players got higher mean scores as compared to the ball games players on these two traits of personality, i.e.; dominance and emotional stability, It means that the combat sports players were found to be better on these traits, but in case of all other traits, both ball games and combat sports players were at the same level. The combat sports players need to be more aggressive, dominant and self-assertive. Moreover they have to be emotionally balanced and mature in order to show their optimum performance in the competitions.

While considering the comparison between ball games and combat sports players for inter-college and inter-university level female sports-persons separately, the results revealed that significant differences existed between ball games and combat games female athletes of inter-college level competition on sociability, dominance, extraversion, conventionality, self-concept and emotional stability as well as internal and external locus of control, but not in case of mental toughness. On all these traits, combat sports players were getting higher mean scores than the ball games players and hence the former were found to be better on all these personality characteristics. But on internal and external locus of control, ball game players were found to be more internally and externally oriented than combat sports players. Usually, it has been observed that individual sports players develop all these personality traits, because they have to perform at their own potential level and so they have to exhibit prowess, toughness, competitive spirit and moreover, they are less internally and externally oriented. Here the hypothesis of the study that there would be significant differences on personality characteristics between female sports-persons of ball games and combat sports has been accepted.

So far as the female sports-persons of inter-university level were concerned, it has been seen that ball games and combat sports players differed on sociability, conventionality, self-concept, mental toughness and external LOC, but not in case of dominance, extraversion, emotional stability and internal LOC. Here the results were contrary to the previous ones, as the ball game players of inter university level were getting higher mean scores on all these above given traits as compared to the combat sports players. But on external LOC, combat sports players scored more than ball games players and hence more externally oriented. The hypothesis of the study that there would be significant differences on the personality characteristics of female sports-persons of ball games and combat sports was partially accepted and partially rejected by the findings of the present study. Dalbara and Singh (2015) in their study, concluded that school level male and female players of individual games differed significantly on sociability, whereas those of team games differed on mental toughness and emotional maturity. College level male or female players of individual games differed on emotional stability and team games female players differed on sociability, whereas university level male and female differed on mental toughness in case of individual games and team games differed on extraversion, mental toughness and emotional stability.

4.12 COMPARISON AMONG FEMALE SPORTS-PERSONS OF DIFFERENT GAMES ON PERSONALITY CHARACTERISTICS

Another objective of the study was to make comparison among female sports-persons of different games on personality characteristics like dominance, sociability, conventionality, extroversion, self-concept, mental toughness and emotional stability as well as locus of control both internal and external. The different games from which the sample was drawn belonged to baseball, football. handball from the ball games and judo, taekwondo and wrestling from the combat sports.

The results of the study indicated that significant differences existed on the first trait of sociability of inter-college female players. Here sociability means a sociable person is warm, good natured, easy going, ready to cooperate, attentive to people, kindly, trustful, softhearted, adaptable and warm-hearted. It is important trait for athletes in that it implies being generous to team mates and that criticism from others will be accepted in good faith.

While comparing the trait of sociability game-wise, it has been shown that baseball players differed from handball players, football from taekwondo and wrestling players; handball from judo, taekwondo and wrestling players. Their mean scores indicate that wrestling (M=44.86), taekwondo (M=44.74), and judo (M=44.52) got higher mean scores than handball (M=40.36), football (M=42.24) and baseball (M=42.98). It means that the players of individual sports like judo, taekwondo and wrestling were more extrovert and sociable than those of the team game players, because these players have been participating at inter college level and playing games and sports since their school days. The participation in sports helps the players to be more sociable and outgoing.

When female sportspersons of inter-university level were compared on the trait of sociability among the different games, it was found that baseball players differed from those of taekwondo, football from taekwondo and wrestling players; handball players from taekwondo and wrestling players; judo from taekwondo and wrestling players. Their mean scores show that handball (M=44.66), football (M=44.54) and Judo (M=43.32) got higher mean scores than wrestling (M=41.26) and taekwondo (M=40.64). These results are contrary to those of the players of inter college level. It means that with experience in sports settings, personality trait like sociability undergo a change,

The second trait of personality was dominance. Dominance denotes self-assertiveness, hardness and toughness, self-assurance, unconventionality and competitive aggressiveness, seducing, persuading or commanding others. Dominance is characterized by a desire to influence and control one's environment and other people and is linked with the ability for directing and controlling other people through subduing, persuading, seducing or commanding them. On dominance trait of personality, significant differences existed among female players of six games. Baseball differed with judo players; football with judo and taekwondo players; handball with judo and taekwondo players as well as judo with wrestling players. Their mean scores indicate that Judo players (M=43.12) were getting higher mean scores than baseball (M=40.90), football (M=39.38), taekwondo (M=41.48) wrestling (M=40.82).and handball (M=39.46). While comparing their counterparts at inter-university level participation, it was found that no significant differences were elicited in the mean scores of dominance trait of personality among the female sports-persons of six games.

The third trait of personality which was measured in this study was extraversion. Extraversion means outgoing, uninhibited, impulsive, involved in group activities, sociable, being friendly, craving for excitement, and having many social contacts. They stick their necks out and take chances, act on the spur of the moment, are optimistic, aggressive, laugh a great deal, lose their temper easily and are unable to keep their feelings under control.

On extraversion trait of personality significant differences were noticed among the female players of six games participating at inter-college and inter-university level competition. In case of inter-college level female players, baseball players differed with handball players; football with judo, and taekwondo players; handball with judo, taekwondo, wrestling players. The mean scores indicate that the range was between 33.96 to 37.32 which was quite close to each other. It means that extraversion trait was found in all types of players to some extent more or less the same level. When compared this trait of the female sports-persons of inter-university level, it was found that baseball players differed from football and handball players; football from taekwondo, and wrestling players; handball from taekwondo and wrestling players as well as judo from taekwondo players. Their mean scores indicate that handball players (M=37.02), and football players (M=36.96) got higher mean scores than those of taekwondo (M=34.28) and baseball (M=34.76).These results show that extroversion trait of personality was possessed by all the players irrespective of the game to which they belonged.

The next trait of personality was conventionality. Conventionality denotes behaviour such as being alert to proper way of doing things, being very practical, narrowing of interests to immediate problems, being realistic, dependable, sound, being concerned and worried about issues. Many researchers have found athletes to be highly conservative and conventional in their responses to social situations. On this trait, differences were found to be significant, so far as the female sports-persons of inter-college level competition were concerned. Baseball players differed from football and handball players; football from judo, and wrestling players; handball from judo, taekwondo and wrestling players. The mean scores indicated that scores ranged between 33.62 to 36.60. It has proved that conventionality trait was required in all types of sportspersons, whether they belonged to team games or individual sports or whether they were from ball games or combat sports. When inter university level players were compared on the trait of conventionality, it was found that football differed from taekwondo players; handball from taekwondo players; judo from taekwondo players.

Their mean scores also ranged between 34.04 and 36.68.which is quite close to their counterparts of college level.

Self-concept refers to several kinds of identifiable personality traits such as self-confidence, self-assurance, self-assertiveness, self-esteem, self-regard, self-consistency, self-enhancement, self-respect. What a person perceives of himself and his achievement in life is called self-concept. Self-confidence and self-assurance in athletes are expressed in behavior as cheerfulness, resilience, toughness, placidity, experience, carelessness, vigor, energy, fearfulness and self-security. (Singh & Cheema, 2005). In the case of self-concept, it was found that significant differences existed between the female players of six games of inter-college level competition. Here baseball players differed from football and handball players; football from judo and wrestling players; handball from judo, taekwondo and wrestling players. Their mean scores indicated that the higher mean scores were obtained by wrestling (M=40.28), baseball (M=39.32) and taekwondo (M=39.06) whereas the lowest mean scores were in case of handball (M=36.72) and football (M=37.24), which shows that wrestling players had better self-concept whereas handball players had low self-concept. But self-concept is also an important trait of personality of the sports-persons. While comparing these results with those of inter-university level players, it was seen that significant differences were not statistically significant as F value was non-significant.

Mental toughness indicates that mentally tough athletes can take rough handling; they are not easily upset about losing, playing badly or being spoken harshly to, can accept strong criticism without being hurt and do not need too much encouragement from their coaches. This is also manifested in realistic, self-reliant and cynical behaviours.(Singh & Cheema 2005). In case of mental toughness, differences were not found to be significant statistically among the female sports-persons of six games for the inter-college level competition. But in case of inter-university level competition, differences were found to be significant among the female athletes of six games. Baseball game players differed from handball players; football from taekwondo players; handball from judo, taekwondo and wrestling players as well as judo from taekwondo players.

Their mean scores indicate that the maximum mean scores were obtained by handball (M=41.72), football (M=40.38) and Judo (M=40.08), where as the minimum scores were in case of taekwondo (M=38, 50), baseball (M=39.10) and wrestling (M=39, 24).

Emotional Stability is characterized by maturity, stability quite realism, absence of neurotic fatigue, placidness, unaffectedness, optimism and self-discipline. While on the other hand, emotional instability is characterized by low tolerance of frustration, immaturity, unstability, high excitability, evasiveness, wordiness and neurotic fatigability. There is a high level of anxiety and apprehensiveness, together with diminished activity, lowered self-confidence and a general loss of initiative. The results of the study revealed that in case of emotional stability, significant differences exits among the female sports-persons of six games at inter-college level competition. Here baseball players differed from football, and handball players; football from judo and taekwondo players; handball from judo players and taekwondo players as well as judo from wrestling players. Their mean scores indicated that the same ranged between 38.94 to 43.28 which are at the optimum level It is also an important personality trait which should be helpful in giving their best performance during competition. But in case of the inter-university level female sports-persons, differences were not found to be significant, though their mean scores also at the same level of emotional stability.

The next variable studied was locus of control. The construct of locus of control is a personality dimension involving an individual's perceived control over events happening in his life. People had internal or external L.O.C. People with an internal locus of control tend to believe that their behaviour or abilities effect outcomes and performances in their lives, whereas those with an external locus of control tend to attribute outcomes to outside powers such as destiny, chance, fortune and other people. The athletes with internal locus of control have self-belief and they consider that they have the ability and skill to perform well in the competition, whereas on the other hand the players with external L.O.C. feel that their performance to win or be successful in the competition depends upon luck or chance factor.

In internal locus of control, differences were observed among female sport-persons of six games of inter-college competition. Here baseball players differed from handball and Judo players; football from handball and judo players; handball from judo, taekwondo and wrestling players; Judo from taekwondo and wrestling players. Their mean scores indicated that handball (M=13.24) and Judo (M=11.14) were more internally oriented whereas wrestling (M=7.28) and taekwondo (M=7.38) were less internally oriented. It means that handball and judo game players had more self-belief and self-sufficiency to perform well in their competition. In case of inter-university level female players also differed significantly. Here baseball players differed from handball and judo players; football, handball and judo players from taekwondo players. Their mean scores revealed that taekwondo players (M=12.06) and baseball players (M-10.42) of university level were more internally oriented, whereas handball (M=8.74) and wrestling (M=9.10) were less internally oriented.

In external locus of control variable, significant differences were found among the female sports-persons of six games of inter-college level competition. Here baseball players differed from football and wrestling players; football from handball, judo, taekwondo and wrestling players; handball with wrestling as well as judo from wrestling players; taekwondo from wrestling players. Their mean scores ranged between 22.00 (Taekwondo) and 32.52(football) which means that football players were more externally oriented who believed in their luck, chance and fate factors. On the other hand, taekwondo players were less externally oriented. Even in case of inter-university level female sports-persons of six games, significant differences were calculated, where baseball players differed from handball, and wrestling players; football from handball and wrestling players handball from judo, taekwondo and wrestling players judo from wrestling players as well as taekwondo from wrestling players. Their mean scores ranged between 18.72(handball) to 25.88 (wrestling) which means that wrestling players of inter university level were more externally oriented and handball players had proved to be less externally oriented. Hence the hypothesis of the study that there would be significant differences on the personality characteristics of the female sports- persons of different games both at inter-college and inter-university levels have been accepted by the findings of this study. Of course, Foster (2002) could discriminate between successful and less successful or outstanding players participating in football, basketball and baseball.

4.13 RELATIONSHIP BETWEEN DIFFERENT COMPONENTS OF PERSONALITY CHARACTERISTICS OF FEMALE SPORTS-PERSONS

Another objective of the study was to establish relationship among the different components of all these variables for female athletes at inter-college and inter-university levels. The different components of personality characteristics were sociability, extraversion, dominance, self-concept, conventionality, mental toughness and emotional stability as well as internal and external locus of control. For this purpose, co-efficient of correlations were calculated with the help of Pearson's product moment method for the total sample, and then for the inter-college female sportspersons and inter-university level female sports-persons separately. The results of the study show that all the seven traits of personality have positive and significant relationship with each other. Here sociability has a high correlation with self-concept (r=0.652) and average positive correlation with dominance (r=0.423) Dominance has middle level correlation with self-concept (r=0.433) and lowest with mental toughness (r=0.273). Extraversion has high correlation with self-concept (r=0.573) and low with emotional stability (r=0.405). Conventionality has the maximum correlation with self-concept (r=0.520) and the minimum with mental toughness (r=0.359). Self-concept has correlation with mental toughness (r=0.471) and emotional stability (r=0.430), whereas mental toughness has relationship with emotional stability(r-0,320). These results have indicated that self-concept was very much related to sociability, dominance, extroversion, conventionality, mental toughness and emotional stability. It has established the perfect and positive relationship among the seven traits of personality. These correlations show the intra-group relationship within one test, i.e.; sports-specific personality inventory. The original test has also given high and positive co-efficient of correlations ranging from 0.224 (self-concept and emotional stability) and 0.537 (between sociability and extraversion). The results of the present study have accepted the hypothesis that significant relationship would exist among the seven traits of personality of the female athletes of different games.

But in case of correlations between these seven personality traits and internal and external locus of control, it was found that correlations co-efficient were negative and low and in some cases non-significant. For example, all the personality characteristics like sociability, extroversion, dominance, self-concept, conventionality, mental toughness and emotional stability had negative and low correlation with internal as well as external locus of control. Similarly, internal LOC had also a negative and low correlation with external LOC. It means that no relationship was established between personality traits of the female athletes with their internal and external locus of control. It can be inferred from these results that locus of control is a different personality construct that measures something else. Moreover internal and external locus of control measure different dimensions of behaviour. It is quite obvious that internal and external locus of control measures opposite characteristics of personality. It was predicted that significant relationship would exist among seven traits of personality has been proved true, but not with locus of control. The hypothesis has been accepted in the first case, but rejected in the second case.

The same results were observed in case of female sports-persons of inter-college level competition, while calculating the co-efficient of correlations of seven traits of personality as well as internal and external locus of control variables. There were positive and significant correlations among the seven personality characteristics of female sports-persons of inter-college level. However, the highest correlation was found between sociability and self-concept and the lowest was with sociability with dominance. But self-concept had high and positive relationship with extraversion, conventionality, mental toughness and emotional stability. But in case of correlations between these seven traits of personality and internal and external locus of control were concerned, it has been found that the co-efficient of correlations were negative and low and in some cases non-significant. The same results were concurred as previously, as all these personality traits of female sports-persons of inter-college level had negative and low correlation both with internal and external locus of control. But internal LOC had also a negative and low correlation with external LOC.

The same results were evinced in case of female sports-persons of inter-university level competition, while finding the co-efficient of correlations of seven traits of personality and internal and external locus of control variables. As it has been noticed that positive, high and significant correlations were there among the seven personality characteristics. Self-concept was found to be highly and positively related with sociability, dominance, extraversion, conventionality, mental toughness and emotional stability. But in case of correlations between these seven personality traits and internal and external locus of control, it was found that co-efficient of correlations were negative and low and in some cases non-significant. All these seven traits of personality traits had negative and low correlation both with internal and external locus of control. But internal LOC had a negative and low correlation with external LOC. The same inference can be deduced as in the case of female sports-persons of inter-college level athletes. So the hypothesis of the study that significant positive relationship would exist between various components of these psychological characteristics of the female sports-persons has been accepted in the case of seven traits of personality, but not in case of the locus of control components.

4.14 RELATIONSHIP OF PERSONALITY CHARACTERISTICS WITH LOCUS OF CONTROL

One more objective of the research was to search the differences on the seven personality characteristics between the female athletes with external and internal locus of control. For this purpose, the total sample was divided into two groups on the basis of their scores on locus of control with the median scores. Those who got scores more than the median scores were considered in the group of internal locus of control and those who scored less than the median scores were taken into external locus of control group. In this way, 327 out of 600 female sports-persons were found to be in the group of internal LOC, whereas 273 out of 600 subjects were in the external LOC group. The results of their mean scores differences indicated that significant differences existed in almost all the personality characteristics, except emotional stability where the mean difference was not significant statistically. Their mean scores showed that on all these personality traits, female athletes of internal LOC group were getting higher mean scores as compared to those of external LOC group. It means that those female sports-persons who were internally oriented and those who believe in their abilities were found better on all these personality traits than those with external LOC. These results have clearly established a positive relation with personality traits and internal locus of control construct of personality. The hypothesis of the study that significant differences would exist on seven psychological characteristics among the female athletes with internal and external locus of control was accepted.

In case of the internal and external locus of control female sports-persons of inter-college level competition, the results indicated that significant differences were found only in case of sociability and extraversion trait of personality, where again female players with internal locus of control were found to be more sociable and extroverted than those with external LOC. Even in case of female players of inter-university level competition with internal and external LOC, it was found that significant differences existed in sociability, extraversion and mental toughness, where again, female players with internal LOC were better in these traits of personality. Here the hypothesis of the study that there will exist differences on personality characteristics between female players with internal and external locus of control is partially accepted and partially rejected.

In the end, it may be stated that no significant differences were found between inter-college and inter-university level sports-persons on almost all the personality characteristics except mental toughness and external locus of control. Ball games and combat sports female players also did not differ on many traits of personality except dominance and emotional stability. But the female athletes of six games both inter-college and inter-university level competitions differed with each in many personality characteristics. There was a positive and significant relationship among the seven personality traits of female players but the same was negative and low in case of personality traits and locus of control. The significant differences are found in almost all the personality characteristics except emotional stability between the female athletes with internal and external locus of control.

4.15 TESTING OF HYPOTHESIS

- The hypothesis of the study that there would be significant differences on personality characteristics between the inter-college and inter-university level female sports-persons was rejected by the findings of this study
- The hypothesis of the study that there would be significant differences on different personality characteristics between female sports-persons of inter-college and inter-university levels competition has been accepted.
- The hypothesis of the study that the inter college and inter university players were having the same level of personality characteristics has been rejected.
- The hypothesis of the study that there would be significant differences on personality characteristics between female sports-persons of ball games and combat sports has been accepted.
- The hypothesis of the study that there would be significant differences on the personality characteristics of the female sports- persons of different games both at inter-college and inter-university levels have been accepted
- The hypothesis that significant relationship would exist among the seven traits of personality of the female athletes of different games.
- The hypothesis of the study that significant positive relationship would exist between various components of these psychological characteristics of the female sports-persons has been accepted in the case of seven traits of personality, but not in case of the locus of control components.
- The hypothesis of the study that significant differences would exist on seven psychological characteristics among the female athletes with internal and external locus of control was accepted.

CHAPTER V

SUMMARY, CONCLUSION AND RECOMMENDATIONS

5.1 SUMMARY

The present study deals with some selected psychological characteristics of female sports-persons at different levels of participation. The main objective of the study was to measure the personality characteristics like sociability, dominance, extraversion, conventionality, self-concept, mental toughness and emotional stability as well as internal and external locus of control variables of female sports-persons of inter-college and inter-university levels competition. It was also the purpose to know the differences on these psychological characteristics between the female sports-persons of inter-college and inter-university level competition and also to make comparison between the female athletes of ball games and combat sports at two levels of competition. It also aimed to find out the relationship among the different dimensions of these variables for female athletes at inter-college and inter-university level of competition. The study also wanted to know the differences on all these personality characteristics between the female athletes with internal and external locus of control.

In order to achieve these objectives, a sample of 600 female sports-persons was selected; out of which 300 subjects were those who had participated at inter-college level competition and other 300 subjects were those who competed at inter-university level sports competition. All these sports-persons were from ball games and combat sports. The ball game athletes were taken from baseball, football and handball; whereas combat sports players were from judo, taekwondo and wrestling. The numbers of the female players were selected equally from each game to have the uniformity in the sample. They were administered Sports Specific Personality Inventory devised by Singh and Cheema (2005) to assess their seven traits of personality; e.g.; sociability, dominance, extraversion, conventionality, self-concept, mental toughness and emotional stability. This test consists of 100 items measuring seven personality characteristics of sports-persons. It is quite a reliable and valid test which is being used in India on the sports-persons. For measuring their internal and external locus of control, Locus of Control test constructed and standardized by Hasnain and Joshi (1992) was administered which has 36 items measuring both internal and external LOC. It is also a reliable and valid tool.

After the data collection, the response sheets of all the female sports-persons who participated in the study were scored on the basis of the scoring keys as provided in their respective manuals. The raw scores were statistically analyzed with the help of SPSS software programme of the computer system.

5.2 REVIEW OF RELATED STUDIES

The early literature in sports personology tried to find out personality profiles which are generally associated with specific games. During the late 1960's and 1970's sports psychologists examined such concerns as the personality trait differences between athletes and non-athletes, successful and less successful athletes, playing one position vs. another, athletes participating in team and individual sports and male and female athletes. They were searching for accurate and definite answers to legitimate questions like "what are the truly and relatively enduring personality characteristics within traits that can have powerful effects upon how athletes perceive situation, and how they act in these situations."

Alderman in his 1974 review of studies on sports personology commented that personality traits like sociability, dominance, extraversion, positive self-concept, emotional stability and mental toughness are consistently identified as loading on successful athletic performance. However, he further commented that the personality profiles of athletes based on measurements of the personality traits do not increase our knowledge of the dynamic tendencies which move people to action. They do not give us a picture of the 'whole' person but just segments. Little attempt has been made to show how these traits integrated with each other to cause overt behavior. In order to rectify such inadequacies in sports personality research, attempts have been made to find out direct relationship between personality characteristics and sports performance.

Foster (2002) conducted a study to determine if 16 personality variables as measured by the Cattell's "16 PF" test could discriminate between successful and less successful or outstanding athletes participating in football, basketball and baseball.

Jaskaran Singh (2005) conducted a comparative study of personality make up of winner and non-winner student sportspersons in relation to socio-economic status. The results revealed that: (i) Winner and non winner sportspersons, as a whole, do not differ in their personality make up; (ii) Socio-economic status is not a significant determinant of personality make-up of sportspersons in terms of neuroticism and extraversion, through low SES seems to enhance psychotic tendencies among sportspersons; (iii) The psychotocism among sportspersons has shown a dependence on socio economic status, where low SES acts as a catalyst to increase psychotic tendencies among non winner sportspersons.

Gurdev Singh and Nishan Singh Deol (2009) conducted the study: "A study of personality characteristics of cyclists at various level of performance." The inter-university cycling riders were found to be significantly better than the inter- college cycling riders. The comparison of inter-college and inter-district cycling riders were not found to be significant, the inter-university cycling riders were found to be significant better than the inter district cycling riders.

Neha Garg and Kang (2009) conducted the study: "Personality profile of winner and loser of soccer players. The study concluded that there are significant differences between the personality of winners and losers.

Vealey Robin (2010) conducted a study on "Sports Personology: A Paradigmatic and Methodological Analysis." The results indicated that sport Personology has shifted paradigmatically from the trait paradigm to interactions, but the cognitive interactional approach has overshadowed the trait-state interactional approach. Methodological trends included an emphasis on correlation methods and field research.

Dalbara (2012) concluded in his recent study that no significant differences are found between male and female sports persons on many personality traits except mental toughness; (ii) School level sports persons do not differ on all personality traits, but college level players differ except on sociability; (iii) significant differences are not found between sportspersons and non-sportspersons on many personality traits except emotional stability.

Locus of control was very extensively researched in relation to general cognition, social and political activitism, mutual aid, birth control, health care etc;. Research and theoretical literature indicates that locus of control construct is an important psychological variable and a personality dimension which appears to differentiate individuals according to a generalized belief or expectancy attitude about control, that this expectancy can be measured and that these measures are predictive of behaviour in a variety of circumstances.

Hattie, Marsh, Neil and Richards, (1997) found that at least to some extent, LOC is a response to circumstances. Some psychological and educational interventions have been found to produce shifts towards internal locus of control

Mamlin, Harris (2001) states that males tend to be more internal than females. They further add that as people get older they tend to become more internal people. Terje Manager & Ode Johan Eikeland (2001) found that girls had significantly higher internal locus of control scores than boys. Boys were, however, significantly more internally oriented than girls on a subscale related to the respondents general belief in luck, while girls were significantly more internally oriented than boys on a school effect scale.

Schultz and Schultz (2005) point out significant differences in locus of control which have not been found for adults in a U.S. population. They further said that there may be specific sex based differences for specific categories of items to assess locus of control. For example, they cite evidence that men have a greater internal locus of control for questions related to academic achievement.

Michele Marie Moore (2006) reported by studying achieving gifted (AG), under achieving gifted (UAG), and non gifted (NG) students that under achieving gifted students were more externally oriented than achieving gifted students. She further added that non gifted students were more externally controlled than achieving gifted students. In regard to underachievers, males were more externally controlled than females.

Sukhdeep (2011) in her study concluded that gifted children differed form normal children in the internal and not in external locus of control; where gifted students were better on the internal locus of control than the non-gifted students. No sex differences were there on either external or internal LOC and no differences were found on both LOC between rural and urban students.

Rupinderjit (2012) in her study found that the male students were more internally oriented than the females. There was no difference on locus of control on the basis of location of schools. But the private school students have more internal LOC than Govt School students According to Seema Garg (2016), no differences exist on the internal and external locus of control of school students; on the basis of sex and types of schools; though differences are found between rural and urban school students; urban students are internally oriented and rural students are externally oriented on locus of control.

The results of the study conducted by Surjit and Agyajit (2017) show that on locus of control, athletes and non-athletes differed in the external and not in the internal LOC; where athletes were found to be better in external locus of control than non-athletes. School level athletes and non-athletes also had differences in the external and not internal, where as college level athletes and non-athletes did not differ either in external or internal. Athletes of school level were better in external LOC. Moreover there were no sex differences in internal and external LOC between male and female students whether they were athletes or non-athletes.

5.3 PROCEDURE AND STATISTICAL TECHNIQUES

After collecting the data, the response sheets of these two tests were scored on the basis of scoring keys provided in their respective manuals. The raw scores were statistically analysed. The following statistical techniques were used on the raw data in order to find out the results:

(i) The means, SD, and SE of the scores of all the variables of female sports-persons belonging to different groups were calculated,

(ii) t-ratios were found out in order to know the significant differences in scores of seven traits of personality and two dimensions of locus of control between two groups formed on the basis of types of games, i.e. sportspersons of ball games and combat sports. And also between female athletes of inter-college and inter-university level competition.

(iii) One way analysis of variance (ANOVA) was computed to know the significant differences in the scores of seven traits of personality and two dimensions of locus of control among six groups of athletes.

(iv) Pearson's product moment of correlation was worked out to find the relationships between two variables as well as inter-co-relationship among all these variables under study.

(v) Post-hoc ANOVA was used where it is applicable.

These results were interpreted and discussed by drawing out the tables and graphs. Hypotheses of the study were tested on the basis of previous studies already conducted and available in the literature. Conclusions were drawn and suggestions may be given to chalk out the strategies for the educational and sports programming of inter college and inter university female sport persons.

5.4 FINDINGS OF THE STUDY

From the results of the study, the following findings can be drawn at:

1. The data had a normal distribution, as the values of mean, median and mode were closer to each other. Skewness and kurtosis values also showed the same results. So the distributions on all the personality characteristics of female sports-persons, whether they were of inter-college level or inter-university level competition were almost normal.

2. While comparing female sports-persons of inter-college and inter-university level on personality characteristics, it was found that no significant differences were observed in almost all the personality characteristics between inter-college and inter-university level female sports-persons except mental toughness and external locus of control variables, where the college level female athletes were had better mental toughness and were more externally oriented than university level female players.

3. In the case of baseball female players, no significant differences existed between inter-college and inter-university level players in all the seven personality characteristics as well as internal and external locus of control.

4. Inter college and inter university level female players of football game differed in conventionality, self-concept and external locus of control trait of personality, where inter university level female players were found to be better in conventionality and self-concept and inter college level players were more externally oriented than their counterparts.

5. Handball female players of inter college and inter university level competition differed in sociability, dominance, extraversion, conventionality, self-concept, mental toughness as well as internal and external locus of control traits of personality, but not in emotional stability. Here the inter university level female players were found to be better in the six traits of personality, whereas inter college level female players were more internally and externally oriented.

6. Inter college and inter university level female players of judo did not differ on many personality characteristics, except the dominance trait of personality, where inter college level female players got higher mean score and hence proved to be better in this trait than their inter university level counterparts.

7. The female players of inter college and inter university level competition of taekwondo differed in sociability, dominance, extraversion, mental toughness and emotional stability as well as internal LOC; where the inter college level female players were better in these personality traits, but inter university level female players were more internally oriented.

8. Differences between inter college and inter university level female athletes of wrestling were found only in case of sociability trait of personality and internal LOC, but not in case of all other traits of personality. The inter college level female players were found to be more sociable and inter university level female players were more internally oriented.

9. The differences between female sport-persons of ball games and combat sports were found only in dominance and emotional stability traits of personality, where the combat sports players were more dominant and emotionally stable as compared to those of ball games.

10. In case of the inter-college level competition, female sport-persons of ball games and combat sports differed in almost all traits of personality, e.g.; sociability, dominance, extraversion, conventionality, self-concept and emotional stability as well as both internal and external LOC; where combat sports players were found to be better in these six traits of personality. But on the other handball game players were more internally and externally oriented.

11. In case of inter-university level female athletes, ball games and combat sports players were found to differ in sociability, conventionality, self-concept, mental toughness and external LOC, but not in dominance, extraversion, emotional stability and internal LOC. Here the ball games female players were better in sociability, conventionality, self-concept and mental toughness, but combat sports players were more externally oriented.

12. In sociability trait of personality, female athletes of six games of inter college level differed from each others. Baseball players differed from handball players, footballers from taekwondo players and wrestlers, handballers from judo, taekwondo and wrestling players. Wrestling, taekwondo and judo players were more sociable whereas handball players were less sociable.

13. Female players of inter-college level of six games differed in the dominance trait of personality. Baseball players differed with judo players, football from judo and taekwondo players; handball players from judo and taekwondo players as well as

judo players with wrestlers. Judo and taekwondo players were more dominant; whereas football and handball players were less dominant.

14. In extraversion trait of personality, female players of six games belonging to inter-college level competition differed from each others. Baseball players differed from handball players; football from judo and taekwondo players; handball from judo taekwondo and wrestling players. Judo and taekwondo players were more extrovert and handball players were less extrovert.

15. Inter-college level female players of six games differed in conventionality trait of personality. Here baseball players differed from football and handball players; football players from judo and wrestling players; handball players from judo, taekwondo and wrestling players. Baseball, judo and wrestling players had more conventionality, whereas handball and football players had less conventionality.

16. In self-concept trait of personality, inter-college female players of six games differed from each other. Baseball players differed from football and handball players; football players from judo and wrestling players; handball from judo, taekwondo and wrestling players. Wrestling, judo and baseball players had better self-concept than handball and football players.

17. Female players of six games participating at inter-college level competition did not differ in mental toughness, but they differed in emotional stability, where baseball players differed from football and handball players, football from judo and taekwondo players, handball from judo and taekwondo players and judo players from wrestling players. Judo and taekwondo players were more emotionally stable, whereas handball and football players were less emotionally stable.

18. In internal LOC variable, female sports-persons of inter-college level of six games differed each other. Here baseball players differed with handball players, football with handball, judo players; handball with judo, taekwondo, wrestling, judo with taekwondo and wrestling players. Handball and judo players were more internally oriented whereas taekwondo and wrestling players were less internally oriented.

19. In external locus of control variable, inter-college female athletes of six games differed from each other. Baseball players differed from football and wrestling players; football from handball, judo, taekwondo and wrestling players, handball from wrestling players as well as judo with wrestling players and taekwondo from wrestling players. Here football players were more externally oriented whereas baseball, handball, judo and taekwondo were less externally oriented

20. While comparing the female sports-persons of inter-university level belonging to six games, it was found that they differed in sociability trait of personality. Here baseball players differed from taekwondo players, football from taekwondo and wrestling players, handball from taekwondo and wrestling players as well as judo from taekwondo and wrestling players. Handball and football players were found to be more sociable than taekwondo and wrestling players.

21. But in the dominance trait of personality, inter-university level female athletes of six games did not differ. So they had the same level of dominance trait.

22. Female athletes of inter university level competition of six games differed in extraversion trait of personality. Baseball players differed from football, and handball players, football with taekwondo and wrestling players, handball from taekwondo and wrestling players, as well as judo from taekwondo players. Here handball, football and judo players were more extrovert, whereas baseball and taekwondo players were less extrovert.

23. On the personality characteristic of conventionality, inter-university level female players of six games differed from each other. Football, handball and judo players differed from taekwondo players. Football, handball and judo players had more conventionality than taekwondo players.

24. Inter-university level female sports-persons of six games did not differ in self-concept trait of personality, which means that all the players irrespective of the games had the same level of self-concept.

25. In mental toughness trait of personality, female athletes of inter-university level belonging to six games differed from each other. Baseball players differed from

handball players; football players differed from taekwondo players; handball from judo, taekwondo and wrestling players as well as judo from taekwondo players. In this trait, handball and football players were found to be tougher minded than taekwondo players who were found to be less tough minded.

26. But in emotional stability trait, inter-university female players of six games did not differ from each other which means that all the inter university level female athletes had the same level of emotional stability.

27. In internal locus of control variable, inter-university female sports-persons of six games differed from each other. Baseball players differed from handball players; football, handball and judo players with taekwondo players; as well as taekwondo also from wrestlers. Taekwondo players were more internally oriented and handball players were less internally oriented.

28. In external locus of control variable, inter-university female sports-persons of six games differed from each other. Baseball players differed from handball and wrestling players; football players from handball and wrestling players; handball players from judo and taekwondo and wrestlers as well as judo and taekwondo players from wrestlers. Here wrestlers were more externally oriented than handball players who were less externally oriented.

29. All the seven traits of personality had positive and significant relationships with each other. But in case of correlations between these seven personality traits and internal and external locus of control, it was found that correlations were negative and low and in some cases non-significant. Internal LOC has also a negative and low correlation with external LOC.

30. The same results were observed in case of female sports-persons of inter-college level of competition. There were positive and significant correlations among the seven personality characteristics. But correlation was negative and low between seven personality traits and internal and external locus of control. Internal LOC had also a negative and low correlation with external LOC.

31. The same results were noticed in case of female sports-persons of inter-university level of competition. There were positive and significant correlations among seven personality characteristics. But the correlations were negative and low and in some cases non-significant between seven personality traits and internal and external locus of control. Internal LOC had also a negative and low correlation with external LOC.

32. Significant differences were found in almost all the personality characteristics except emotional stability between female sports-person with internal and those of with external locus of control. The female sports-persons with internal locus of control were found to be better in the first six personality traits than those with external locus of control.

33. In case of the inter-college level female sports-persons, it was found that only in sociability and extraversion traits of personality, there were differences between internal and external LOC female sports-persons. Here again female players with internal locus of control were found to be better in these two personality traits as compared to those with external LOC.

34. In case of inter-university level female sports-persons, significant differences existed in sociability, extraversion and mental toughness personality traits, where again female players of internal locus of control were found to be better in these traits of personality than those of external LOC.

5.5. CONCLUSIONS

From the findings of the study as outlined above, the following conclusions can be arrived at:-

1. No significant differences are found in almost all the personality characteristics between inter-college and inter-university level female sports-persons except mental toughness and external locus of control variables. In case of the games like football, handball, taekwondo and wrestling, the female athletes of inter college and inter university levels differ in some personality traits and external locus of control to some extent.

2. The differences between female sports-persons of ball games and combat sports are found only in dominance and emotional stability, where the combat sports are more dominant and emotionally stable than their ball games counterparts. But in case of inter college level competition, female sports-persons of ball and combat sports differ in almost all traits of personality, where again combat sports players are found to be better in the six traits of personality and ball games players are more internally and externally oriented.

3. In the different traits of personality and locus of control, the inter-college and inter-university female sports-persons of six games, i.e; baseball, football, handball, judo, taekwondo and wrestling differ from each other. Wrestling, taekwondo, judo players of inter college level are more sociable, dominant, extrovert, conventional, have better self-concept, emotionally stable. Handball and judo players are more internally oriented, whereas football players are more externally oriented.

4. In case of inter university level competition, handball and football players are found to be more sociable, more extrovert, tough-minded. But taekwondo players are more internally oriented and wrestlers are more externally oriented..

5. All the seven traits of personality have positive and significant relationships with each other. But the correlations between seven personality traits and internal and external locus of control are negative and low Moreover, internal LOC has also negative and low correlation with external LOC, both in case of female sports-persons of inter-college and inter-university level competitions.

6. Significant differences are found in almost all the personality characteristics except emotional stability between female sports-persons with internal and those with external locus of control. The female sports-persons with internal locus of control are found to be better in the first personality trait than those with external locus of control.

5.6 RECOMMENDATIONS FOR FUTURE RESEARCH

1. After undergoing the present research work, the investigator faced many research hazards and thought of many other research problems which can be taken up by the future research students and research scholars in the field of physical education and sports psychology.. The following suggestions are being put forward which may be considered for future researchers.

2. This research work has been conducted on the female sports-persons of inter college and inter university level competition. So there is a need to conduct this type of work on the school level sports-persons, who are the budding players in the field of sports.

3. The present study was confined to the female sports-persons. The research should also be done on the male sports-persons, so that a comparison may be done on gender basis. The male and female differences on all these variables may be found out.

4. In the present study, the female players of ball games and combat sports have been investigated. So there is a need to conduct research work on the players of individual and team games to find the differences on different psychological variables.

5. Here personality traits of female sports-persons have been studied. There are many other psychological variables which need to be investigated for the players e.g.; self-efficacy, self esteem, emotional intelligence and self-concept etc.

6. Sports-Psychology can play an important role in the present scenario for enhancement of sports performance of our sports-persons. Psychological skills training is the need of the hour. So research should also be conducted on different psychological skills e.g.; imagery, motivation techniques, stress management techniques, goal setting and self-confidence etc.

BIBLIOGRAPHY

Aamodt, M., Alexander, C., & Kimbrough, W. (1982): -Personality characteristics of Skills, 55,327-330

Acompora, B (1971): - A comparison of Personality traits among three of female field hockey competitors. Unpublished Master'thesis, Deptt of Physical Education, SanJose College, San Jose, California.

Alderman, R.B. (1974): Psychological Behavior in Sports. Philadelphia, W.B. Saunders Co.

Allen Edward John (1982): "definition of Locus of control", Central will retrieve.

Allport, G.W. (1961): -Pattern and growth in Personality. New York: Holt Rinehart Winston.

Annastasi, A (1954): Psychological Testing, Macmillan Publishing Co, New York.

Archer, J. (1994): Achievement goals as a measure of motivation in university students, contemporary Educational Psychology, 19, P 430-446.

Argyle, M & B.R. Little (1972):-"Do personality traits apply to social behavior." Journal for the Theory of Social Behavior, 2, Pp.1-35.

Argyle, M. (1975):- Personality and Social Behavior. In B.R. Little (ED.), New perspectives in personality. Harmpndsworth: Penguin Books.

Ashu Jain (2012):- Locus of control and Self-concept of high school Students in relation their perceived Self-Efficacy and Emotional Intelligence. Unpublished PhD thesis Singhania University. Pacher Bari (Rajasthan).

Bandura, A. (1977): - Social learning theory. Englewood Cliffs, NJ: Prentice Hall.

Bandura, A (1977):-Self-efficacy: Toward a unifying theory of behavioral change. Psychological Review, 84; 191-225.

Bandura, A (1982):-Self-efficacy mechanism in human agency. American Psychology, 37:122-147.

Bandura, A (1986): Social foundations of thought and action: A social cognitive theory. Englewood Cliffs, N.J.: Prentice Hall.

Bandura, A., & Walters, R. H. (1963): *Social learning and personality development*. New York: Holt, Rinehart, & Winston.

Battle, E.S. and Rotter, J.B. (1963): "Children's feelings of personal control as related to social class and ethnia group". J. pers, 31: P 482-490.

Berger, B.G (1970):-"Effect of three sport environmental factors upon selected personality characteristics of athletes." Unpublished Doctoral Dissertation, Columbia University.

Berger, R.A.& Littlefield, D.H. (1969): -Comparison between football, athletes and non-athletes on Personality. Research Quarterly, 40:663-665.

Berhram, R.M & Kroll, W (1967): -Personality differences between non-swimmers and swimmers. Research Quarterly, 38:163-171.

Best, John W & Kauh, James V (2008): Research in Education (10th Ed.) New Delhi: Pearson Education Inc.

Bhargava, M (2006): Modern Psychological Testing and Measurement. Agra: H.P. Bhargava Book House.

Bhattacharya, Mousumi; Dutta, Ashok; Mandal, Manas K. (2004). "Factor Structure of Emotional Intelligence in India", Psychological Studies. Vol.49. Nos. 2-3, 142-146.

Bhatti, A.S. (1987):-Psychological and anthropocentric differentials of athletes and non-athletes. Unpublished PhD thesis, Kurukshetra University, Kurukshetra.

Bhullar, J (1981):-A comparative study of attitudes towards physical activity of high and low intelligence groups of university students,Vyayam Viduyan,14 (1 & 2), 12-15.

Bhullar.J (1974):-Personality adjustment of sportsmen and non-sportsmen. International Journal of Sports Psychology, 5:2:111-116.

Bialer, I. (1961): "Conceptualization of Success and Failure in Mentally Retarded and Abnormal Children," J. Pers., 29, p. 303-332.

Biddulph, Lowell (1954): - "Athletic Achievement and the personal and Social Adjustment of high School Boys", Research Quarterly, 25:1-7.

Billey (1971): Primer of Educational Research by Newton, Sutor, USA.

Bird, E.L. (1970): -"Personality structure of Canadian intercollegiate women ice hockey players." In G.N.Kenyon (Ed.) Contemporary Psychology of Sport. Chicago: Athletic Institute, pp-149-156.

Bird, E.L. (1978): -The Q-sort method in personality assessment and psychiatric research. Palo Alto, Ca, consulting.

Block, J (1971):-Lives through time, Berkley, California: Bancraft Books.

Block, J (1978):-Advancing the psychology of personality: paradigmatic shift or improving the quality of personality at the crossroads: current issues in interactional psychology. Lawrence Erlbaum Associates, Hillsdale, New Jersey, Pp.37-64.

Booth, E. G. (1958): "Personality Traits of Athletes as measured by the MMPI".Research quarterly, 29(1)127-138.

Bredemeier, B, & Shields, D (1986): Athletic aggression: An issue of contextual morality. Sociology of Sports Journal, 3, 15-28.

Bredemeier, B. (1978): Assessment of reactive and instrumental athletic aggression. *Proceedings of International Symposium on Psychological Assessment.* Wingate Institute of Physical Education and Sports, Israel.

Brewer, B.W., Van Realte, J.L.; Linder, D.E. & Van Realte, N.S. (1991): Peak performance and the perils of retrospective introspection. Journal of Sport & Exercise Psychology, 13,227-238.

Broady, L.E. & Benhaw G.P. (1986): Social and emotional adjustment of adolescents extremely talented in verbal or mathematical reasoning. Journal of Youth and adolescence 15(1), 1-18

Brown, R.T. (1980): "Locus of control and its relationship to intelligence and achievement", Psychological Reports, 46(3, Pt.2), 1249-1250.

Bruner, B.C. (1969): - Personality and motivating factors influence adult participation in vigorous physical activity. Research Quarterly, 40: 464469.

Burdashaw, D (1971):-Personality profile of non-swimmer among University women. International Journal of Sports Medicine & Physical Fitness.11:2:80.

Burley, R.C. Turner, L.A. and Vitulli, W.F. (1999): "The relationship between goal orientation and age among adolescents and adults," The journal of Genetic Psychology, 160, P 84-89.

Bushan, S & Aggarwal, V. (1978): -Personality characteristics of high and low achieving Indian sports persons. International Journal of Sports Psychology,9(3);191-198.

Buss, D.M. (1991): Evolutionary Personality Psychology." Annual Review of Psychology: 42.

Callini, James V. and Kantorowski, L.A. (1982): "Internal-External Locus of Control." New Normative Data, Psychological Reports (August), 5(i): p. 231-235.

Cardi, M. (1962): An examination of internal V/s eternal control in relation to academic failure. Unpublished Masters Thesis, Ohio State University, 1966.

Carmen, L.R; Zerman, J.L and Blainc, G.B.(1968): Use of the Harvard Psychiatric Service by athletes and non-athletes. Mental Hygiene, 52: 134-137.

Cattell, R.B. (1956):-Personality and motivation theory based on structural measurement. In J.L. McCary (Ed.) Psychology of Personality, New York: Grove Press.

Cattell, R. B. (1965): - The scientific analysis of personality. Baltimore: Penguin

Cattell, R.B. (1960): Some psychological correlates of physical fitness and physique. In Exercise and Fitness in the modern world. Chicago: The Athletic Institute.

Cattell, R.B. (1964): Hand Book for the 16PF Questionnaire Champaign: *IPAT.*

Chadwick, Ida, F (1972): -A comparison of the personality traits and kinesthetic augmentation and reduction of college female and non-athletes. Dissertation Abstracts International, 33, 1005 A, 1006 A,

Chance J.E. (1965): “Internal Control of reinforcements and the school learning process”, Paper presented at the Biennial meeting of the society for research in child development, Minneapolis.

Chaudhary, N (1986):- Emotional maturity as a correlate of the mental health of adolescents staying at home and orphanages. Journal of Indian Education.60-65.

Cheek, J.M. (1982):-Aggregation, moderator variables and the validity of personality tests: A peer rating study, Journal of personality and Social Psychology, 43, Pp, 1254-1269.

Coleman, M.R. (1966): Recognizing social and emotional needs of gifted students, Gifted child today magazine, 19(3), 36-37. EJ5 2762.

Conroy, D.E. & Benjamin, L.S. (2001):-Psychodynamics in sport performance enhancement consultation: Application of an interpersonal theory. The Sport Psychologist, 15,103-117.

Cooper, L. (1969): - “Athletics, Activity and Personality: A Review of Literature”, Research Quarterly, 40:17-82.

Cox, R.H. (1998):-Sport Psychology: Concepts and application (4th ed.)Boston: WCB/McGraw-Hill.

Crandal, V.J; Katkovsky, W and Preston, A (1962): “A conceptual formulation for some research on children's achievement development”, Child Development, 33, p. 643-661.

Crandall, V.C., Kotkovsky, W. and Preston, A. (1965): "Motivational and ability determinants of young children's intellectual academic situations." Child development, 33, p. 643-661.

Cratty, B.J. (1989): -Psychology in Contemporary Sport (Third edition).Englewood Cliffs, NJ Prentice Hall.

Daino, A (1985): -Personality traits of adolescent tennis players. International Journal of sport Psychology, 16(2), pp 120 -125.

Dalbara & Singh Agyajit (2015):-Sports Personology: A study of Indian Sports-persons. Twenyfirst Century Publications, Patiala.

Dalbara, Singh (2012):- A comparative Study of Sports Personology of Indian sportspersons at different levels of participation. Unpublished PhD thesis. Jodhpur National University, Jodhpur.

Dardin, E (1972): - Sixteen Personality Factors profiles of competitive body builders and weightlifters. Research Quarterly, 43:142-147.

Davies, D (1989):-Psychological factors in competitive sport. London: Falmer Press.

Davis, C (1992):-Body image, dieting behavior and personality factors: A study of high performance female athletes. International Journal of Sports Psychology, 23(3):179-192.

Davis, W. L. and Phares, E.J. (1967): Internal-external control as determinant of information seeking in a social influence situation." J. Pers., 35; 547-567

Demane, A and Devisse,T (1987): Locus of control, mental ability, self-esteem and alienation." Social behaviour and Personality, 15(2): 233-236.

Dewan, R (1996): The socio-economic status and social maturity. The Progress of Education, LXXIII (5), 117-119.

Diener, E; R.J Larson & R.A. Emmons (1984):-"Person x situation interactions: choice of situations and congruence response models." Journal of personality and social Psychology, 47, 5, pp80-592.

Dishman, R.K.(1982):- Contemporary sport psychology. Exercise and Sport Science Reviews, 10,120-159.

Dole, S. (2000): "The implications of the risk and resilience literature for gifted students with learning disabilities", Roeper Review, 23(2), p. 91-97.

Douglas, P & Powers, S. (1982): "Relation between achievement, locus of control and expectancy of success of academically gifted high school students", Psychological Report 51 (3 Pt. 2) 59-1262.

Dowd, R and Innes, J.M. (1982): -Sport and Personality: Perceptual and Motor Skills, 53, 79-89.

Duda, J.L. (1992): Motivation in Sport Setting: A goal perspective approach. In G.C.Roberts (Eds.), *Motivation in sport and exercise* (Pp.57-91) Champaign, IL: Human Kinetics.

Dureha, D.K. (1986): -Comparison of personality characteristics of sportsmen and non sportmen.Paper presented at national sports conference at Gwalior. National Sports Conference, Nov.1986.SNIPES Journal, (2):3-6.

Dureha, D.K. (1987): "Comparison of personality characteristics of sportsmen and non-sportsmen." SNIPES Journal, Vol.10.1 &2 Pp.26-30.

Edwards, A.C. (1959): Manual of Edward's Personal Preferences. Schedule, New York: *Psychological Corporation.*

Ellison, K. & Freischlag, J. (1975): -"Pain Tolerance, Arousal, and Personality Relationships of Athletes and Non athletes". Research Quarterly, 46: 250- 255.

Endler, N.S. & D. Magnusson (1974):-Interactionism, trait psychology, psychodynamics and situationism. Reports from the Psychological laboratories, the University of Stockholm, No. 418.

Endler, N.S. & Hunt, J.Mc V and Rosenstein, A.J. (1962):-As S-R Inventory of Anxiousness. Psychological Monographs, 1962, 76, N 017 (1-33)

Endler, N.S. (1973):-"The person versus the situation—a pseudo issue? A response to Alker."Journal of Personality, 41, Pp287-303.

Endler, N.S. (1975):- A person-situation interaction model for anxiety. In C.D. Spielberger and I.G. Lara son (Eds) "Stress and Anxiety" Vol 1, Washington: Hemishere, Pp145-164 (a).

Endler, N.S. (1977):-"The case for person-situation interactions." Canadian Psychological Review, 16, 12-21, (b).

Endler, N.S., & Magnusson, D. (1976): - Interactional psychology and personality. New York: Wiley.

Eysenck H. (1960): -The structure of Human Personality. London: Routledge.

Eysenck, H.J. & Eysenck, S.B.G. (1968):- Eysenck Personality Inventory Manual. London: University of London Press.

Eysenck, H.J. (1960): - The effects of psychotherapy. In H.J.Eysenck (Ed.), Handbook of abnormal psychology: An experimental approach. New York: Basic Books.

Eysenck, H.J. (1963):-On the dual nature of extraversion. British Journal of Social and Clinical Psychology, 2:46-55.

Eysenck, H.J. (1967): - The Biological basis of Personality. Springfield, Illinois, Thomas.

Eysenck, H.J. (1968):-Manual for the Eysenck Personality Inventory. San Diago. California Educational and Industrial testing Services.

Eysenck, H.J. (1969):-Scores of three personality variables as a function of age, sex and social class. Brit Jr.Soc.Clin.Psychology.8 (1) 69-76.

Eysenck, H.J. (1970): - The structure of human personality (3rd ed.), London: Methuen.

Eysenck, H.J.(1965):-"Extraversion and the acquisition of eye blink and GSR conditional responses."Psychol Bull, 63,258-70, 51, 52,131.

Eysenck, H.J., Nias, D.K.., & Cox, D.N. (1982): -Sport and personality. Advances in Behavioral Research and Therapy (An International Review Journal) Vol 4(1): 1-56.

Fazel A, (1995): A Study of cultural and Gender differences on need for achievement, Locus of control and vocational choices of gifted and average students. Unpublished Ph.D. thesis in Psychology, Panjab University, Chandigarh

Finchman, F & Barling, J. (1978): "Locus of control and generosity in learning disabled normal achieving and gifted children". Child Development, 49, 330-333.

Fisher, A.C (1984):- New directions in sport personality research. In J.M. Silva & R.S.Weinberg (Eds.): Psychological foundations of sport (pp.70-80), Champaign, IL: Human Kinetics.

Fisher, A.C. & Zwart, E.F. (1982): -Psychological analysis of athletes' anxiety responses. Journal of Sport Psychology.4, 139-158.

Fisher, A.C. (1976):-Psychology of sport: Issues and Insights. Palo Alto.CA, Mayfield.

Fisher, A.C. (1978):-"Multidimensional scaling of sport Personality data: An individual differences approach." Journal of Sport Psychology.1: Pp.76-86.

Fletcher, (1971): - Relationship between personality traits and high school activity participation. Psychology, 8, 40-43.

Foster (2002): "A Discriminant analysis of selected personality variables and motor ability of players and non players." International journal of sports physiology. P.No.221.

Foster, E.G.(1972):-Personality traits of highly skilled baseball and softball women athletes. Dissertation Abstracts. International: 39 (9A): 5055.

Foster, W.C. (1969): - A study of the Personality characteristics of female athletes and non-participants. Master's thesis, University of Oregan.

Frank.N.P (1989):- Personality profiles of athletes and non-athletes in developing countries. Journal of Physical Education and Sports Sciences. Gwalior.

Franklin, R.D. (1963): Youth's expectancies about internal v/s external control of reinforcement related to N-variables Dis. Abs. Int. 24, 1684.

Fraziwer, S.E. (1986):-Psychological characteristics of male and female marathon runners of various performance levels. Dissertation Abstracts International, 47(6) 2976-A.

Freedson, P.S., Mihevic, P., Loucks, A., & Girandole, R.(1983):- Physique, body composition and psychological characteristics of competitive female body builders. The physician and Sports Medicine, 11,85-90,93.

Freeman, F.S. (1962):-Psychological Testing. Holt Rinehart, New York.

Fridhandler, B.M. (1986):-"Conceptual note on state trait and the state-trait distinction." Journal of Personality and Social Psychology, 50,169-274.

Giges, B (1998):-Psychodynamic concepts in sport psychology: Comments on Sean and Sean (1998). The Sport Psychologist, 12,223-227.

Gill, D. (1986): Competitiveness among females and males in physical Activity Classes, Sex Roles, 15, 233-247.

Gill, D. (2000): - Psychological dynamics of sport and exercise. Champaign, IL: Human Kinetics.

Gill, D.L. & Deeter, T.E. (1988):- Development of the sport orientation questionnaire Research Quarterly for Exercise and Sport, 59,191-202.

Golas, R, W. (1971): -"A comparative study of two personality dimensions in athletes and non-participants." Paper presented at the meeting of the Eastern District Association for Health, Physical Education and Recreation, Philadelphia,

Gormly,J (1983):-"Predicting behavior from personality trait-scores." Personality and Social psychological Bulletin, 9,267-270.

Graves, T.D. (1961): "Time perspective and the deferred gratification pattern in tri-ethnic community Denver", University of Colorado, Institute of Behavioural Science.

Grossarth-Maticek, R; H.J. Eysenck, H, Reider and L. Rakic (1990):- Psychological factors as determinants of success in Football and Boxing: Effects of Behavior Therapy.

Gruber, J, & Perkins, S (1978):- "Personality traits of women physical education majors and non-majors at various levels of athletic competition." International Journal of Sport Psychology, 9(1): 40-52.

Guilford, J.P. (1959): - Personality. New York: McGraw-Hill.

Gupta, V.P. & Sharma, T.R. (1976):-Personality characteristics of University athletes and non-athletes. Indian Journal of Applied Psychology, 13:97-99.

Gupta, V.P. (1972): Personality Characteristics of Participants in individual and team sports as measured by Sixteen Personality Factor Inventory. *NIS Journal*, 2 (2): 33-37.

Gurdev Singh and Nissans Singh Deol (2009): "A study of personality characteristics of cyclists at various level of performance" Souvenir of 3rd National conference on Opportunities & Challenges in Physical Education, Pbi. Uni. Patiala, PP.6

Haertel, G.D., Walberg, H.J. and Wang M.C. (1990): "What influences learning. A content analysis of review literature," Journal of Educational Research, 84, P 30-43.

Hall, C.S & Lindzey, G (1979):- Theories of Personality. Wiley Eastern Limited, New Delhi.

Hasnain, N & Joshi, D.D. (1992): Manual for Locus of Control Scale. Lucknow, Incur Psychological Agency.

Hattie, J.A., Marsh, H.W., Neill, J.T & Richards, G.E. (1997): Adventure Education and Outward Bound: "Out-of-class Experiences that have a lasting effect", Review of Educational Research, 67, p. 43-87.

Hein, M (1954): -A comparison of certain personality traits of college women to selection of activities for physical education instruction. Master's thesis, women's college. University of North Carolina.

Hendry, L.B. (1970): Some notion on personality and sporting ability: Certain comparisons with scholastic achievement. Quest 13, 63-73.

Heusner, M.V (1952):-Personality traits and champion athletes. Unpublished M.A. thesis. University of Illinois.

Hollander, E.P. (1967): - Principles and methods of Social Psychology. New York: Holt, Rinehart, & Winston.

Horn, T.S. & Hashrook, C.A. (1987): Psychological characteristics and the criteria children use for self-evaluation. *Journal of Sport Psychology*, 9, 208-221.

Howe, B.L. (1976): Achievement and Affiliation in Sports for Junior and Senior School athletes. *Proceedings of Svetouy Kongress, ISSP, Prah*

Hung, Y. (1982): "Psychological Characters among the mentally retarded and gifted students in junior high schools", Bulletin of Educational Psychology 15, 167-193.

Hunt, D.H (1969): -A cross-racial comparison of personality traits between athletes and non-athletes. Research Quarterly, 40; 704-707.

Ibrahim, H (1967): -Comparison of temperament traits among inter-collegiate athletes and physical education majors. Research Quarterly, 38:615-622.

Ikegami, K (1970):-Character and personality changes in the Athletes. Contemporary Psychology of Sports. Chicago: Athletic Institute.

Ikegami, K. (1968): "Character and Personality changes in the Athletes", In G.S. Kenyon, (Ed.). Contemporary psychology of sport. Second International Congress of Sports Psychology. Chicago: Athletic Institute. Pp 51-60.

James, W.M. (1957): "Internal Versus external control of reinforcement as a task valuable in learning theory," unpublished Doctoral Dissertation, Ohio State University.

Jaskaran Singh (2005): "A comparative study of personality makes up of winner and non-winner students sportspersons on Sports Psychology, Dr. Ambedkar College, Nagpur.pp.25.

Johnson, A.P. (1951):-Notes on a suggested index of item validity: The U-L Index. Journal of Educational Psychology, 42: 499-504.

Johnson.P.A (1972): -"A comparison of Personality traits of superior skilled female athletes in Basketball, Bowling, Field Hockey and Golf." Research quarterly, 43Pp 409-415.

Kalliopuska, M (1998):-Personality and motivational factors of the top athletes. Paper presented in the International Congress of Psychology. Montreal, Canada.

Kames, Frances A; Mc Ginnis, J. Christopher (1996): "Self - Actualization and locus of control with Academically Talented Adolescents," Journal of Secondary Gifted Educaiton, V7n2 P 369-72.

Kamlesh, M.L, and Kaur, A. (1986): *Self-esteem in Physical Education majors with regard to their course-placement. Abstract-cum-Souvenir.* Second National Conference of Physical education and Sports Sciences, Patiala.

Kamlesh, M.L. (1985):-Track and Field athletes on the anvil of A-S Reaction Study. Journal of Sports, Physical Education and Sports Sciences.8 (2), 17-23.

Kamlesh, M.L.(1982):-A comparative study of high and low performers in athletics on some selected variable of personality. Unpublished PhD thesis Punjabi Uni. Patiala.

Kamlesh, M.L.(1982):-A comparative study of high and low performers in athletics on some selected variable of personality. Unpublished PhD thesis Punjabi Uni.Patiala.

Kamlesh, M.L.(1984):-A comparative Study of extraversion and neuroticism in track and field athletes. Research Biannual for Movement.13 (1) 8-19.

Kamlesh, M.L.: Singh, Balbir and Kaur,K. (1984): A peep into personality variables with regard to prospective physical education teachers. *SNIPES Journal 7(4), 42-48.*

Kane, J, E, (1965): -Personality profiles of physical education students compared with others. In Ferruccio Antonelli (ed.) Proceedings of First International Congress of Sports Psychology, 1:772-723.

Kane, J.E (1967): -The description of sport types using the 16 PF. Research in Physical Education. I, I. London, Physical Education Association.

Kane, J.E. (1964): -Personality and Physical ability. International congress of Sport Science. Proceeding Tokyo, Japan

Kane, J.E. (1966): -Personality description of soccer ability. Research in Physical Education.1, 1.

Kane, J.E. (1966): -Psychological correlates of physiques and physical abilities. In International Research in Sport and Physical Education (Ed.) E.Johl and E.Simons.Springfield, P85-94.

Kane, J.E. (1968): -Personality and physical Abilities. In G, S Kenyon, (ed.) Proceedings of the second International Congress of Sport Psychology, 131-141, Chicago Athletic Institute. Kenyon.

Kane, J.E. (1968):-"Personality in relation to physical ability and physique."Ph.D thesis, University of London.

Kane, J.E. (1970): - Personality and physical abilities. Contemporary Psychol. Sport, Chicago: Athletic Institute.

Kane, J.E. (1970):-Psychological aspects of physical education and sports. London. Routledge and Kegan Paul.

Kane, J.E. (1971):-"Personality description of soccer ability." Res. In Phys.Edu, 1, 54-64.

Kane, J.E. (1972): -Psychological aspects of sports with special reference to the female. In D.Harris (Ed.), women and Sport: A national Research conference. The Pennsylvania state university, University Park, Pa.

Kane, J.E. (1980):-"Personality research: The current controversy and implications for sport studies." In W.F. Straub (Ed.), Sport Psychology: An analysis of athletic behavior (2nd Ed.)Pp.228-240 Ithaca, NY: Movement Publications.

Kane, J.E. (Ed.), (1966): - Readings in physical education. London: P.E. Association

Karnes F.A., D' llio V.R. (1991): "Locus of control in rural southern elementary gifted students", psycho rep, 69 (3 pt 1); P 927-8.

Kavussanu, Maria & Robert, G.C. (1996): Motivation in physical activity contexts: The relationship of perceived motivational climate to intrinsic motivation and self-efficacy. *Journal of sport & Exercise Psychology,* 18, 264-280.

Kaur, G (1984):-A comparative study of personality characteristics of participants and. Patiala non-participants in physically activity groups. Unpublished Master thesis, Punjabi University.

Kelley, S.L. (1975):-Personality characteristics of female high school athletes. Physical Fitness Research Digest Series 5(3).

Kenrick, D.T. & Springfield, D.O. (1980):-"Personality traits and the eye of the beholder. Crossing some traditional philosophical boundaries in the search for consistency in all of the people." Psychological Review, Pp.87, 88-104.

Kesar, S.P. (1980): "Locus of control among high and low achievers at different levels of economic status." M.Ed. Dissertation

Killick, Lawrence Alan (1999): "The effects of gender and ethnicity upon locus of control of gifted grade 8 students". http://hdl. handle.net/2429/9657.

King, P.J & Peter, C.S. (1975):-Personality and athletic. Social structure. Psychological Abstract, 55(2), 31-32.

Kirkcaldy, B.D. (1982): "Personality and Sex differences related to positions in team sports." International Journal of Sport Psychology.13 Pp 141-153.

Knight, Bruce Allen (1995): "The Influence of Locus of control on gifted and talented students," Gifted Education International, V_{11} n_1 P31-33.

Kroll, W. & Carlson, R.B. (1967): -"Discriminant Function and Hierarchical Grouping Analysis of Karate Participants' Personality Profiles." Research Quarterly, 38: 405-411.

Kumar, A & Thakur, G.P. (1986): -"Extraversion, Neuroticism and Psychoticism in Athletes and Non-athletes." In N.N. Mall and J.Mohan (Ed.) Psychological Analysis of Sports Performance. Gwalior, LNCPE, 34-36.

Kumar, A; Pathak, N & Thakur, G.P. (1985): Mental health of individual, team and non-athletes. Proceedings of VI world conference in Sport Psychology, Denmark..

Ladwing, G.W. (1963): "Personal, situational and social determinants of Preference for delayed reinforcement", Unpublished doctoral dissertation, Ohio State University.

Lakie, W.L. (1962) Personality characteristics of certain groups of inter-collegiate athletes. Research quarterly, 33:p556-573.

Lazarus, R.S., & Monat, A. (1979): - Personality (3rd ed.), Englewood Cliffs, NJ: Prentice-Hall.

Leary, M.R. (1992): Self-presentational processes in exercise and sport. *Journal of Sport & Exercise* Psychology, 14, 339-351.

Lefcourt, H.M. (1976): Locus of control, New York: Halsted Press.

Lefcourt, H.M. (1976): Locus of control, New York: Halsted Press.

Levy, L.H. (1970):- Conceptions of personality: Theory and research, New York: Random House.

Little, J.C (1969): -The athlete's neurosis-A deprivation crisis. Acta. Psychiatrica Scandinarica. 45:187-197.

Liverant,S and Scodal, A (1960): Internal and external control as determinants of decision making under conditions of risk. Psychological Reports, 7:59-67.

Long, Vonda, O. Martinez, Estella, A (1994): Masculinity, femininity and Hispanic professional women's self-esteem and self acceptance. Journal of Counseling and development, 73;183-186.

Luthar, S.S. (1991): Vulnerability and Resilience: "A Study of High Risk Adolescents", Child Development, 62, 600-616.

Lynne, J.H. (1980): "A Comparison of the locus of control of children in the gifted and average ranges of intelligence". Distt. Abs. Int. 40(8-A), 4467.

Maddi, S.R. (1976):- Personality theories: A comparative analysis. Homewood, IL: Dorsey press.

Maddux, J. (Ed.) (1995): "Self efficacy, adaptation, and adjustment Theory, research and application," New York: Plenum.

Magnusson, D & Endler N.S. (1977):-Personality at the crossroads: Current issues in international psychology. Lawrence Erlbaum Associates, Hilsdale, NJ.

Mahoney, M.J.: Gabriel, T.J. and Perkins, T.S. (1987): Psychological skills and exceptional athletic performance. *The Sports Psychologist*, 1, 181-199.

Malhotra, M.S. and khan, H.A. (1984): Personality traits of Experienced coaches, *SNIPES Journal* 7 (4). 32-37.

Malumphy, T (1968): - Personality of women athletes in Inter-collegiate competition. Research Quarterly.39 (No.3): 610-620.

Mamlin, N., Harris, K.R., Case, L.P. (2001): "A Methodological Analysis of Research on Locus of Control and Learning Disabilities: Rethinking a Common Assumption", Journal of Special Education Winter. http://wilderdom.com/ psychology/loc/locus of control what IS.? Html.

Marten, R.: Vealey, R.S. & Burton, D. (1990): Competitive anxiety in sports (Pp. 3-115); Champaign, IL: Human Kinetics Publishers, Inc.

Martens, R & Peterson.J.A. (1981):-Group cohesiveness as determinant of success and member satisfaction in team performance. In John, W, Loy, G.S. Kenyon and B.D. Mcpherson (Eds.) Sports Culture and Society: A reader on the sociology of sports. Lea and Fibiger, Philadephia.

Martens, R (1975):- The paradigmatic crisis in American Sport personology, Sportwissenschaft, 5, 9-24.

Martens, R (1977): Sport Competition anxiety test. Champaign, IL: Human Kinetics.

Martens, R; Burton, D; Vealey, R.S., Bump, I.A & Smith, D (1982): Cognitive and somatic dimensions of competitive anxiety (CSAI-2) Paper presented at NASPSPA conference. University of Maryland, College Park

Martin, F., & Lumsden, J (1987):- Coaching: An effective behavioral approach. St.Louis: Times Mirror/ Mosby.

Martin, K.A. & Mack, D. (1996): Relationship between physical self-presentation and sport competition trait anxiety: A preliminary study. *Journal of Sport & Exercise Psychology,* 1, 75-82.

Mayer, David and Calkin (1979): "Academic achievement, self-concept in locus of control," A casual analysis of longitudinal study

McClelland, DC (1973). Human Motivation. London: Cambridge University Press

McClelland, DC (1991): Human Motivation. London: Cambridge University Press

McGhee, P.E. and Crandall, V.C. (1968): "Beliefs in Internal Control of Reinforcement and Academic Performance", Child Development. 39, p. 91-102.

Mckelvie, S.J. & Husband, D.E. (1980): -A locus of control and anxiety in college athletes and non-athletes. Perceptual and Motor Skills, 50:810-822.

McNair, D; Lorr, M; & Droppleman, L (1971): Profile of mood states manual. San Diego: Educational and Testing Service.

Mehrabian, A., & Bekken, M.L. (1986): - Temperament characteristics of individuals who participate in strenuous sports. Research Quarterly for Exercise and sport.57, 160-166.

Melind, A., Solmon and Amelia M.Lee (1997): Cognitive Processes Questionnaire in Physical Education (CPQ PE). Development of a instrument to assess cognitive processes in physical education Classes. *Research Quarterly For Exercise and Sport*, Vol. 68, No.2, 152-160.

Meredith, G.H & Harris, M.M.(1969):-Personality traits of college women in beginning swimming/Perceptual and Motor Skills 29:216-218.

Michele Marie Moore (2006): 'Variations in Test Anxiety and Locus of control orientation in Achieving and underachieving gifted and Non-gifted Middle School student', A Ph. D Dissertation at the University of Connecticut

Mischel, W & Peake, P.K.(1982):-"Beyond idea in the search for cross- situational consistency." Psychological Review, 89, Pp730-755

Mischel, W (1968):-Personality and assessment. New York: Wiley.

Mischel, W (1969):-Continuity and change in personality. American Psychologist, 24, Pp, 1012-1018.

Mischel, W (1971):-Introduction of Personality, New York: Holt, Rinehart and Winston.

Mohan & Kaur, P. (1986): Standardization of Personality Questionnaire EPQ on Indian students. Journal of Personality and Clinical Studies, 2:127-133.

Mohan, J, Sehgal, M & Khan, H.A. (1992): Personality dimensions in sportsmen and non-sportsmen, In J, Mohan; N.K.Chadha & S.Akhtar (Eds.) Psychology of Sports: The Indian Perspective, Friends Publications, Delhi.

Mohan, J. (1989): Personality and Sports Excellence, Paper presented at 15th Sea Games Seminar, 15-17 Aug., Kuala Lampur.

Mohan, J; Mall, N.N. & Paul, V.P. (1979): -"Comparative study of Extraversion, Neuroticism and Attitudes towards Sports of Handball players and non-players." SNIPES Journal, 2:1.

Moore, J.T. (1973): Personality variables between female high school inter-school sport participant. Master, Thesis, Spring Field College, Physical Fitness Research Digest, 3, 14.

Morgan, W.P. (1980):- Psychological benefits of physical activity. In F. J. Nagle & H.J. Montoye (Eds.) Exercise in health and disease. Springfield, IL: Thomas.

Morgan.W.P. (1979):-Prediction of performance in athletics. In P. Klavora & J.V. Daniel (Eds), Coach, athlete and the Sport Psychologist (pp.173-186), Champaign, IL: Human Kinetics.

Murray, H.A, (2006):-Exploration in Psychology, New York: Oxford University Press.

Murray, H.A. (1938): Explorations in Psychology, New York: *Oxford University Press.*

Mushier, C.L. (1970): -"A cross-sectional study of the personality factors of girls and women in competitive lacrosse." Unpublished doctoral dissertation. University of Southern California, Los Angles.

Mushier, C.L. (1970): -"A cross-sectional study of the personality factors of girls and women in competitive lacrosse." Unpublished doctoral dissertation. University of Southern California, Los Angles.

Neal, P.E.(1963);-Personality traits of united states women athletes who participated in the 1959 pan-American games as measured by the Edwards Personal Preference Schedule. Unpublished Master's thesis. University of Utah, Salt Lake city.

Neha Gang and G.S.Kang (2009): "Personality profile of winner and loser of soccer players" Souvenir of 3rd national conference on Opportunities & Challenges in Physical Education, Pbi. Uni. Patiala, pp.9.

Newman, E.N. (1968): -Personality traits of faster and slower competitive swimmers. Research Quarterly, 39:1049-53.

Niblock, M.W. (1960): -Personality traits and intelligence level of female athletes and non-participants from McNally High School, Doctoral Dissertation, Pennsylvania State University.

Nideffer, R.M. (1976): The inner athlete. New York: Crowell.

Ogilvie, B.C (1968): -Psychological consistencies within the personality of high-level competitors. Journal of the American Medicine Association.No.205, 156-162.

Ogilvie, B.C (1971): -Encyclopedia of Sport sciences and Medicine. New York: Macmillan.

Ogilvie, B.C. (1973): -Working on he mind: The swimmers magazine, Acquative world, 15-16.

Otten (1977): "Inventory and expressive measures of locus of control and academic performance" a 5 year outcome study.

Ozer, D.J & Gjerde, P (1989):-Patterns of personality consistency and change from childhood through adolescence.J.Pers.57, Pp483-507.

Persone, D.R. (1964): -Personality traits of national representative swimmers of Canada, 1962.Unpublished Master's thesis, University of British Columbia, 1963.Completed Research in Health, Physical Education and Recreation, 6; 44.

Pervin, L.A. (1968):-"Performance and satisfaction as a function of an individual-environment fit." Psychological Bulletin, 69, Pp, 56-68.

Peterson, S.L., Weber, J.C., & Trousdale, W, W. (1967): - Personality traits of women in team sports vs. women in individual sports. Research Quarterly for Exercise and Sport, 38,686-690.

Phares, E.J (1968):-Locus of control in personality, Morristown, NJ: General Learning Press

Phares, E.J. (1955): Perceptional threshold decrements as a function of skill and chance expectancies. J. Psychol. 53, p. 399-407

Piedmont, R.L., Hill, D.C. & Blanco, S. (1999): - Predicting athletic performance using the five-factor model of personality. Personality and Individual Differences, 27,769-777.

Pierce, R.A. (1969): -Athletes in Psychotherapy: How many, how come? Journal of American College Health Associaion.17; 244-249

Prufrock, Cross, T.L. (2004): "On the social and Emotional Lives of Gifted Children.

Pyecha, J (1970): -Comparative effects of judo and selected physical education activities on male university freshman Personality traits. Research Quarterly, 41:425-431.

Ramsay L.M. (1962): -A comparison of the Personality variables and attitudes towards Physical Education between highly skilled girls participating in varsity program and girls athletic Association Program. Master' thesis, women college, University of Carolina.

Rao, S and Murthy, V.N. (1984): Psychological correlates of locus of control among college students. Psychological studies, 29(1):51-56.

Reeds, G.K.(1999):-Prediction of performance from selected personality traits and state anxiety levels of competitive male and female gymnasts. Dissertation Abstracts international, 45(8), 2441-A.

Rishi, P.J. (2007): "Questioning the utility of Self-efficacy Measurements for Indians". The entity from which ERIC acquires the content, including journal, organization and conference names, or by means of online submission from the author, International Journal of Research and Method in Education, 30(2), p. 193-206.

Ritchie, E and Phares, E.J. (1969): Attitude change as a function of internal-external control and communicator status. J.Pers, 37:429-443.t5

Robert J. Vallerand; Balnehard Celine, Provencher Pierre and Briere M., Nathalie (1997): Development and Validation of the Multidimensional Sportspersonship. Orientation Scale, *Journal of Sport & Exercise Psychology,* 19, 197-206.

Rotter, J.B (1966): Generalized expectancies for internal versus external control of reinforcement. Psychological Monographs, No 609, 1-28.

Rotter, J.B. (1954): Social learning and clinical psychology. Englewood Cliffs, N.J. Prentice-Hall.

Rotter, J.B. (1990): Internal versus external control of reinforcement. American Psychologist: 45, 489-493.

Rotter.J.B. Chance, J. E and Pharos's. J (1972): Application of a Learning Theory of Personality. New York: Holt, Rinehart and Winston.

Roul, U (1998):-Sports and Personality. New Delhi, Northern Book Centre.

Ruffer.W.A. (1965): - A study of extreme physical activity groups in young men. Research Quarterly, 36:183-195.

Rupinderjit (2012): Emotional Intelligence of Adolescent Children in relation to Locus of Control, Emotional Maturity and Academic Achievement. Unpublished PhD thesis submitted to Singhania University, Pacheri Bari.

Rusch, J.M. (1972): -Personality traits and sports participants of adult women. Unpublished Master thesis. University of Texas.

Rushall, B.S. (1967): -Personality profiles and a theory of behavior modification for swimmers. Swimming techniques, 4:66-71.

Rushall, B.S. (1968):-An investigation of relationship between personality variables and performance categories in swimmers. International Journal of Sports Psychology, 1:93-104.

Rushall, B.S. (1970): - "Some Practical Applications of Personality Information to Athletics", in Gerald S. Kenyon, Ed, Contemporary psychology of sport: Second International congress of sport Psychology. Chicago: Athletic Institute. Pp 167-174.

Rushall, B.S. (1972): -"An evaluation of the relationship between personality and physical performance categories. In G.S.Kenyon (ed.)"Proceedings of 2nd International congress of Sports Psychology. Athletic Institute, Chicago.

Sahni, P.Sood & Mohan, J (1988): A comparative study of sportsmen and non-sportsmen of university level. Proceedings of the Scientific Journal of Sports, Patiala.

Sahota, Ajit Singh (1989): Evolution of Sport Specific Personality Inventory for Use in Sports. M.A. thesis, N.I.S. Patiala.

Sandhu, G.S., Mann, N.S & Brar, R.S.(1987): Comparative study of extraversion, neuroticism and attention of team and individual athletes. In L, S.Sidhu and D.N.Mathur (ed.) Sport Sciences: Health, Fitness and Performance, Patiala.IASSPE, 233-236..

Schendel, J (1965): -Psychological differences between athletes and non- athletes in athletics at three educational levels. Research Quarterly, 36(1), 52-67.

Schultz, D.P., Schultz, S.E. (2005): "Theories of Personality (8th Ed.) Wad worth", Thomason. ISBN 0-534-62403-2.

Schwarzer, R. (1994): Optimism, Vulnerability and self beliefs as health-related cognitions; A systematic overview, Psychology and Health, An international Journal, 9, P 161-180.

Schwenkmerge, P, & Laux. (1986): Trait anxiety, worry and emotionality in athletic competition. In C.D.Spielherge and Diaz, R. Guerdon (Eds.), Cross-cultural anxiety, Vol.3, 65-78. Washington, B.C.: *Hamisphere Publishing Corporation.*

Seema Garg (2016):- Locus of Control of High School Students of Punjab State in relation to their Perceived Self-Efficacy and Emotional Intelligence.Ph.D thesis in Education submitted to Desh Bhagat University, Mandi Gobindgarh.

Seifriz,J.J.; Duda, J.L.; & Chi,L. (1992): The relationship of perceived motivational climate to intrinsic motivation and beliefs about success in basketball, *Journal of Sport & Exercise Psychology*, 14, 375-391.

Shanker, G (1986): -"Personality of Indian varsity male gymnasts." In: N.N.Mall and J.Mohan (ed.) Psychological Analysis of Sport Performance, Gwalior, LNCPE.

Sharma, R.K. (1999):-A comparative study of personality of athletes belongs to various sports and games. Indian Journal of Sports Studies, 1-5.

Sharma, S.S. & Shukla, B.R K (1986): -"Psychological study regarding personality characteristics of individual and team sports." SNIPES Journal, 9, 3, Pp.36-42.

Shurr, K.T; Ashley, M.A & Joy, K.L.(1977): A multivariate analysis of male athletic characteristics: Sport type and success. Multivariate Experimental Clinical Research, 3:53-68.

Silva J.M. & Weinberg, R.S.(1984):-Psychological Foundations of Sports. Champaign: IL: Human Kinetics Publishers.

Silva, J.M. (1984): -"Personality and sport performance. Controversy and challenge." In J.M. Silva and R.S.Weinberg (Eds). Psychological Foundations of Sport. Champaign, IL: Human Kinetics Publishers

Silva,J.M.,Schultz,B.B.,Haslam,R.W;Martin,T.P.&Murray,D.F.(1985):- Discriminating characteristics of contestants at the United State Olympic Wrestling trial. International Journal of Sport Psychology, 16:79-102.

Singer, R, N. (1974): -Physical Education: An Integrated Approach. New York: Holt Rinehart and Winston.

Singer, R.B. (1972):- Coaching, Athletics and Psychology. New York: McGraw- Hill co.

Singer, R.N. (1967): -Athletic participation: Cause or result of certain personality factors. Physical Education.24; 169-171.

Singer, R.N. (1968):-Motor Learning and human performance, New York: Macmillan.

Singer, R.N.(1982):-What Sports Psychology can do for the athletes and coach. International Journal of Sports Psychology, vol, 15.pp, 52-61.

Singh, A.J. (1986): "Psychological characteristics of top level Indian sportspersons." In L.S.Sidhu and D.N.Mathur (Ed.) Sport Sciences: Health Fitness and Performance. Patiala, IAOSSPE pp231-232.

Singh, A.P. & Singh, S (1986): "Anxiety. Neuroticism and Extraversion among the cricket players and non-sportsmen. "In Psychological Analysis of Sports Performance(Ed) N.N.Mall and J.Mohan, Gwalior, LNCPE, 48-55.

Singh, Agyajit & Cheema, H.S. (2005):- Sports Specific Personality Test. National Psychological Corp. Agra.

Singh, Agyajit (1992): Sports Psychology: A study of Indian sportsmen, New Delhi, Friends Publications.

Singh,A.J.(1986):-"Psychological characteristics of top level Indian sportspersons." In L.S.Sidhu and D.N.Mathur (Ed.) Sport Sciences: Health Fitness and Performance. Patiala, IAOSSPE pp231-232.

Slusher, H.S.(1964): Personality and intelligence characteristics of selected high school athletes and non-athletes. Research Quarterly, 35:539-545.

Smith, R.E.; Schultz, R.W.; Smoll, F.L., & Packed, J.T. Multidimentional measure of Sport-specific Psychological Skills: The Athletic Coping Skills Inventory-28. *Journal of Sport & Exercise Psychology*, 17, 379-398.

Sowa, C.J. Mclntire J., May K.M. and Bland, L., (1994): "Social and emotional adjustment themes across gifted children," Roeper Review, 17, P 95-98.

Sperling A.P. (1970): - "The relationship between Personality Adjustment and Achievement in Physical Education Activities." Research quarterly, 13:351-363.

Strean, W.B.; & Strean, H.S. (1998):-Applying psychodynamic concepts to sport psychology practice. The Sport Psychologist, 12,208-222.

Sukhdeep Kaur (2011): Emotional Intelligence of Gifted Students in relation to their Locus of Control and Self-Efficacy. Unpublished PhD thesis submitted to Singhania University, Pacheri Bari.

Surjit Singh & Agyajit Singh (2015):- A comparative study of locus of control between athletes and non-athletes. at different level of participation. Indian Journal of Psychology. Vol 27. 3.

Surjit Singh & Singh Agyajit (2017):- Psychological Characteristics of Sports Persons: An Indian perspective.IAHRW Publication Pvt. Ltd. New Delhi.

Surjit Singh (2014):- A Study of Psychological Characteristics of Athletes and Non-Athletes at Different Level of participation. Unpublished PhD thesis. Singhania University, Pacheri Bari.

Surjit Singh (2015). A study of Psychological Characteristics of Athletes and Non-Athletes at Different level of Participation. In Agyajit Singh & Urvashi Roul (2015) (Ed.) Sports Psychology in India: An Empirical Journey. New Delhi. Northern Book Centre

Terje Manger, Ole-Johan Eikeland (2001): "On the relationship between locus of control, level of ability and gender, Scandinavian Journal of Psychology, V.41, issue 3, P: 225-229.

Thakur, G.P. & Ojha, M (1981): -"Personality differences of Indian table tennis, badminton and football players on primary source traits in the 16 P.F."International Journal of Sport Psychology, 12"196-203.

Thakur, G.P. & Thakur, M (1980): - Personality differences between the athlete and non-athletes college males." International Journal of Sport Psychology, Vol II, 3, p.180.

Thorndike, R.L & Hagen, E (1955): Measurement and Evaluation in Psychology and Education. New York: John Wiley & Sons.

Tillman, K.G. (1964):-The relationship between physical fitness and selected personality traits. Dissertation Abstracts, 25:276-277.

Tutko, T. & Richard, A (1971):-Anxiety in L.H.Larson (Ed.) Encyclopedia of Sports Science and medicine, New York: Macmillan.

Tutko, T., Lyon, L.P. and Ogilvie, B. (1969): Athletic Motivation Inventory Sanjose: Institute for the study of athletic motivation.

Valliant, P.M.; Simpson-Housley, P; McKelvie, S.J (1981):-Personality in athletics and non-athletic college groups. Perceptual and Motor Skills, 52:963-966.

Vanschoyck, S, R. & Grasha, A.F. (1981): Attentional style variations and athletic ability: The advantages of a sports-specific test. Journal of Sport Psychology, 3,149-165.

Vealey, R. (2001):-Understanding and enhancing self-confidence in athletes. In Resigned, H.Hausenblas, & C. Janelle (Eds.) Handbook of sports psychology (2nd ed.pp-550-565). New York: Wiley.

Vealey, R. (2010):-Understanding and enhancing self-confidence in athletes. In R.Singer, H.Hausenblas, & C. Janelle (Eds.) Handbook of sports psychology (2nd ed.pp-550-565). New York: Wiley.

Vealey, R.S (1989): Sports Personality: A Paradigmatic and Methodological analysis. Journal of Sport & Exercise Psychology (JSEP), 11 (2), 216-235.

Vealey, R.S. (1986):- Conceptualization of sport-confidence and competitive orientations: Preliminary investigation and instrument development. Journal of sport psychology, 8,221-246.

Vealey, R.S. (1992):-Personality and Sport: A comprehensive View. In T.S. Horn (Ed.), Advances in Sport Psychology. Champaign IL: Human Kinetics.

Vealey, R.S.(2002):-Personality and sport behavior. In T.S.Horn (Ed.) Advances in sport psychology (Pp.43-82) Champion IL: Human Kinetics.

Vernon, P.E. (1964):-Personality assessment: A critical survey. New York: Wiley.

Warburton, R.W., & Kane, J.E. (1966): - Personality related to sport and physical ability. In J.E.Kane (Ed.), Readings in physical education. London: P.E. Association.

Warburton, R.W., & Kane, J.E. (1966): Personality related to sport and physical ability. In J.E.Kane (Ed.), Readings in physical education. London: P.E. Association.

Weber, R.J (1953):-Relation of physical fitness to success in college and personality. Research Quarterly, 24; 4:470-474.

Weinberg, R & Genuchi M (1980): -: Relationship between SCAT, state Anxiety and Golf Performance. A Field Study." Journal of Sport Psychology, 2, 2.

Weinberg, R.S. & Gould, D (2007):- Foundations of Sport & Exercise Psychology (4th Ed). Champaign IL, Human Kinetic

Weinberg, R; Reveles, M. & Jackson, A (1984):- Attitudes of male and female athletes towards male and female coaches. Journal of Sports Psychology, 6,448-453.

Weiner, Bernard (1973): "Success and Failure as Motivators in class Room", Belton: Brooks Col.

Werner, A.C., & Gottheil, E. (1966): -Personality development and participation in collegiate athletics. Research quarterly, 37:126-131.

Whiting A.T.A., Stembridge, D.E. (1965):- Personality and the persistent swimmer. Research Quarterly, 36:348-356.

Williams J.M. (1970):-Principles of physical Education. Philadelphia, W.B. Saunders & co.

Williams, I., Gill, I.D. (1995): 'The role of perceived competence in the motivation of physical activity. *Journal of Sport & Exercise Psychology*, 17, 363-378.

Williams, J.M & Widneyer, W, N, (1991):-"The cohesion-performance outcome relationship in a co-acting report." Journal of sport and exercise psychology, 13(4)1, Pp364-372,417.

Williams, J.M. & Hoepner, B.J; Moody, D.L. & Ogilvie, B.C.(1970):-"Personality traits of champion level female fenders." Research Quarterly, 41.pp446- 453.

Williams, J.M. (1978): -"Personality characteristics of the successful female athletes." In Straubs W.F. (Ed)'Sport Psychology: An Analysis of Athletic Behavior.(2nd ed. P.353-359)Ithaca ,NY:Mouvement Publications.

Williams, J.M. (2001): - Applied Sports Psychology: Personal Growth to Peak Performance. (4th Ed.) Mountain View, CA, Mayfield. Pub. Co.

Wright, J.C. & Mischel, W (1987):-"A conditional approach to dispositional constructs: The local predictability of social behavior."J. Pers. Soc. Psychol, 53, Pp301, 22,418.

Yang Fuyi, Liang Ningjian (2005), A Research on Problem Student's Implicit Self-esteem, Department of Psychology, East China Normal University, Shanghai, Psychology Science.

Yeater, Julia (1977): -"The psychology of coaching: The personality of the female basketball." Kellogg's coach of the year clinic Manual.Telecoach Inc, Pp222-226.

Zanna, M.P.; Olson, J.M & Fazio, R, H, (1980):-"Attitude-behavior consistency—An individual difference perspective." Journal of personality and Social Psychology.Pp38, 432-440.

Zimbardo, P.G. (1985): Psychology and life. Glenview. IL: Scott Foreman and Company

CPSIA information can be obtained
at www.ICGtesting.com
Printed in the USA
LVHW021429011222
734355LV00016B/903

9 781805 459798